INDIVIDUAL ADVANTAGES

FIND THE I IN TEAM

Dr. Brian Smith

ISBN 978-1-54394-634-5 eBook 978-1-54394-635-2

TABLE OF CONTENTS

0.0

Editor's Preface

I CAN HONESTLY SAY THAT THIS BOOK BEGAN AT THE PERFECT time in my life. This book has helped me on my journey to live more intentionally, take notice of life, and appreciate the good and the bad. Each of us is experiencing life in a vastly different way from the person next to us; we have different experiences, personalities, jobs, habits, friends, morals, characters, attitudes, maturity, goals, will power, failures, successes, languages, environments, beliefs—there are more things than can be named that make us all individual. But we have one thing in common with every other person in this world: We are all human.

To live this human experience is a gift. To share our human experience through writing is an even greater gift. Telling stories to teach, to provoke laughter, sadness, anger, even to frighten, is a tradition older than recorded history. We communicate through stories that tap these emotions. Communication through emotion is something that can be understood by all humans, regardless of the boundaries of language. This book brings you that kind of communication.

Individual Advantages: Find the I in Team communicates lessons and philosophies through the rawness of emotions and the stories tethered to them. My dad has created a book in which you can see his real human experience and what he has learned from battles we all face. He tackles some of life's hardest questions: "Who am I?" and "What is my purpose here?" Through stories, he will give you the tools he has successfully used so that you may also tackle some of these questions.

To have the ability to learn from others' mistakes and successes is a privilege many of us take for granted. There have been many instances in my life when I have learned from others' human experience, and I am certain that there have been many instances when others have learned from mine. While you may have picked up this book thinking it would be a conventional self-help book or a business guide, you will be surprised to find that it is so much more.

This is not an ordinary self-help book. I have found that too often in self-help books I am instructed on what I need to do in order to get to my desired destination, and I am told what I am doing wrong with my life. Too often, self-help books only provide an answer to questions or a solution to problems that we may face; they do not show us the means by which they came to these conclusions. This way of teaching is superb in some areas of learning, but for the complexities of our human experience, it does not measure up.

Our lives are far too dynamic individually, let alone when you consider the 7.6 billion other experiences that humankind has every day. We have been learning from one another for millennia through stories. This book brings us back to that type of learning: the learning needed to understand and comprehend some of life's greatest questions.

Being the daughter of someone who not only lives by these philosophies but also teaches them has given me a great advantage. Some of my dad's colleagues have described me as a "case study" for this book. What

I have learned from my dad and his teachings goes far beyond anything I could put into words. He has taught me how to love, forgive, move on, have grace, be fierce, stand up for what I believe in, be a great team member, and hold myself accountable. Above all else—what I truly cherish most—he taught me how to empathize.

I was lost for so long before my dad started writing this book. The kind of lost where you honestly believe you may never find yourself again. The kind of lost that makes you question who you are and what you're really doing here. Being a part of the writing of this book helped me find myself again. It allowed me to rediscover my foundation, the foundation my parents spent so long building and worked so hard to build for me as a child. It allowed me focus on my life's mission: To make this world a better place for all living beings.

The benefits you will get from this book will go beyond the excitement of reading stories that provoke various emotions; you are being given the opportunity to learn and to better yourself. You will be able to analyze yourself more clearly and with less bias. This book will prepare you to be your best self with each team you influence: family, friends, coworkers, and strangers. I wish for you a prosperous life.

0.0

Acknowledgements

I WAS UNSURE WHERE THIS BOOK PROJECT WOULD TAKE ME. The title changed a few times as we got deeper into the concept. As the first book of three, this is a testament to our philosophy: Individual Advantages. I wouldn't have been able to finish this project without the influence of my amazing team; their support propelled me. Our company, IA Business Advisors (IA = Individual Advantages), is filled with people who exemplify the core philosophy of this book.

I owe thanks to my family for all things in my business life. My wife, René—who has been my rock since the day we met—influences me to work hard, and the pride this instills in me gets me through each day. Our success as businesspeople, parents, and friends is grounded in our partnership, our marriage, and our friendship.

My three children grew to be a part of that rock, too. Kristin, my older daughter, is one of my inspirations; she repeated a lot of the lessons I learned throughout life and managed to create a good life for her family as I did for mine. My granddaughter, Kenzi, is a tremendous source of pride for me, and Kristin's husband is someone I am proud to call family.

Henry, my youngest, is as stubborn as kids come. Through it all, he has remained true to his goals and beliefs. As we button up this first book, he is headed off to college through a Navy ROTC scholarship. He is taking his next step toward fulfilling his life-long dream of being a naval officer.

Then there is Mary. Mary is my middle child, and together we wrote this book. Yes, 98 percent of the words are mine, but without Mary, this book would not be. It has been a pure joy to work with her, and I look forward to whatever the future holds as we continue to develop the lessons taught in these pages.

Recognizing those who have helped me get here doesn't repay all that I owe them. Their efforts are unparalleled. Spencer, while attending law school and working a full-time job, read and reread this book to ensure that its lessons were cohesive and clear. Braden provided amazing insight into many of the lessons and challenged me to dig deeper into my thoughts and memories to ensure that the lessons resonated with my intention. Sarah and Jerrod read and reviewed chapters and provided context and imagery that will serve to bring a little visual connection to the words. And Hannah (after I shared this book concept with numerous professional graphic designers) designed a concept for the cover that perfectly captures the meaning of this book.

I also recognize my parents and siblings. First, my mother has been a positive influence on my life since high school. Prior to high school, I think all our lives were just organized chaos, created by young parents struggling to raise young children; today my mother is one of my best friends and my stepfather, Jeff, is like a father to me. You won't hear much about my father or stepmother in this book; they certainly had an influence on who I am, but we have not had anything close to a child-parent relationship since the late 1980s. I am happy that their marriage has lasted over thirty years and they managed to raise three children of their own. Then there are my siblings: Becky, Justin, Brandt, and Alexandra. Becky, with whom

I share both parents, like my mother, is a good friend, and she and Chris (my brother-in-law) are truly amazing people. I don't really know my other siblings, born to my stepmother, well, but I am happy to know that they are all successful and happy in their own way.

To name the remaining individuals who have influenced me on the journey to writing this book would take a book of its own. The people in my stories who have influenced me in my lifetime contributed to the lessons that have made me a better person. I am eternally grateful for the good and bad that has happened. They have provided me with the opportunity to create for you a book of lessons taught through stories. I hope they will help you Find the I in Team.

0.0

Introduction

"The most difficult thing is the decision to act, the rest is merely tenacity. The fears are paper tigers. You can do anything you decide to do. You can act to change and control your life; and the procedure, the process is its own reward." - Amelia Earhart

THIS BOOK WILL BE A JOURNEY OF AND ABOUT YOU. AS YOU will see, each of us is the most important person to ourselves, just as you should be the most important person to yourself.

We will map that journey and explore the advantages of the individual. It is our philosophy that the word *individual* has a dual meaning: one person/many persons, one action/many actions, one word/many words. One is an individual; collectively, they are Individual. Throughout this book, you will notice the use of this term and the subtle differences in its usage. When referring to a single person, task, or action, the word *individual*—with a lowercase *i*—will be used. When referring to an entity that is made of multiple individuals, the word *Individual*—with a capital *I*—will be used.

There is a word that I am notorious for using, even when it seems I am clearly speaking about myself alone: We. I have been known for using the word *We* when speaking about my own work. This is because there haven't been many things in my professional career that I alone have provided; I always have a team supporting me. From my education (both formal and through experience), to the support I get in the office, from partners and vendors, or from my family, there is always a We for me. The habit of recognizing my teams has provided for me a working relationship with people around the world for over 22 years. To this day, I still correspond and work with people who were peers, partners, vendors, employees, and customers back when I began my career journey. I am We, and all that I have become is due to the We in my life. What about your life: Who is your We?

What this book will not be is another self-help book that leaves you wondering, *Can I really do this?* There are no disclaimers such as "results are not typical." This book is about self-realization. It can only fail you if you fail to be honest with yourself. Other books require that you measure up to others: make more money, be more successful, lose more weight, be a better husband or wife. Individual Advantages is about you and how you influence others; those results are subjective to you and those people alone. It's about understanding yourself and that influence, not about measuring yourself against others or some generally accepted attribute. If you apply the concepts in this book, you will have an epiphany about how your own individual advantages will affect the advantages of other individuals; you will have the ability to affect and manage change with any individual or Individual you influence.

We will also help you to define prosperity in your life. Prosperity as defined generally today means certain wealth: financial, emotional, romantic, platonic, professional, educational. I would argue that prosperity is none of these things. I have met people with none of these things who feel prosperous and I have met people with all of these things who are not satisfied with their place in life. Prosperity is personal to each and every one of us and is part of the Individual Advantages equation that you will come to understand by the end of this book.

We intend to give you the tools necessary not only to learn and apply the philosophies taught here, but also to apply the philosophies you have learned in the past. How many books/seminars/videos/podcasts have you read/been to/studied/listened to? How many years have you been trying to better yourself or your company through these media and seen no improvement? I don't say this to disparage the great work done by the people who themselves have developed or identified ways by which people can make themselves better. However, many of the programs, practices, or philosophies being taught don't resonate beyond the initial excitement of hearing the words of or reading about the success of others.

It is also important to know that we will be asking you to look at yourself without rose-colored glasses. You cannot be your best for others if you are not your best for yourself, and that means being honest with yourself. Too often we make excuses that we think are only detrimental to ourselves, but every time we lie or allow ourselves to fall short of personal goals, we chip away at that person who is an advantage to everyone we individually influence. Self-realization, which we will guide you toward, may be difficult. You will see how for me it opened memories I had long suppressed. If those memories cause you anxiety or any other type of negative feelings, it's important that you seriously think about sharing them with someone close to you whom you trust or a psychologist; to realize your full individual advantage, you will have to realize the foundation of who you are.

This act of self-reflection will require a thoughtful approach, as you will require from yourself, internally, the truth. For things we do not know that require more than intuitive knowledge, the only way to gain complete understanding is to slow down. It is also during these times of self-reflection that we may experience internal fear of learning. We are humbled by what we uncover about ourselves; to know truth about our individual is to remove those rose-colored glasses. The realization that we are individually alone and Individually together influences each of us.

1.0

Meet Individual Advantages

"Remember always that you not only have the right to be an individual, you have an obligation to be one." - Eleanor Roosevelt

L ET ME BEGIN BY SHARING THE STORY OF HOW INDIVIDUAL Advantages (IA) became what it is today. Individual Advantages has been the name of my company since 1996. My inspiration for the name has escaped many people through the years, including my wife, René. In fact, she recently told me that for the first twenty-one-plus years of our company's existence she misunderstood the name. This revelation came during one of our morning coffee conversations while we were discussing the title of this book.

While I have always understood the meaning behind the name Individual Advantages, we have often struggled to have a solid identity because of this name. Countless people have said to me, "Can you not create a better brand than 'Individual Advantages'?" Even more frustrating was the confusion on people's faces when I explained what Individual Advantages was: *a company that helped other companies understand the correlation of people, process, and technology, and the advantages each of these individually has within the workplace.* This was how I explained the name in the early years. Looking back on this explanation, it still makes sense to me, though now I understand why people would look at me with confusion in their eyes.

In the early years, I found it difficult to create our best public image while still keeping the true meaning of IA. For me, Individual Advantages was never about a name but about my belief in what actually makes companies viable: the individual. Through the years, I played around with names and logos that I hoped would help our clients and potential clients realize who we are and what we do. While doing this, we as a company (Individually) continued to apply our tried-and-true approach to solving business problems posed to us by clients; creating advantages for them continued to be the end result.

The other names we tried never captured the true message of IA; in fact, I felt those names lost a certain amount of who we were as an organization. In the mid-2000s, we tried Business Efficiency Group. While that name said, in part, who we are and that we help businesses, it did not express our beliefs. In 2009, we again tried a new brand: YourBizDr.Com. This brand did get quite a bit of hype, and its success has paved the way for this book to be written and for me to share the true value of who we have always been: one of many Individual Advantages for our clients.

The name YourBizDr.Com came from my close friend Kevin, who called me the "Biz Doctor" and suggested that we could apply our practices via virtual services to more people. And so we did. From 2009 to 2014 we helped over eighteen thousand business owners, managers, and employees realize their individual advantages all through virtual services. However, each time I found our company falling back to our foundation: Individual Advantages. In 2014, when we had the opportunity to sell our virtual consultancy, I was relieved. It's hard to consult to such a large group of clients and affect viable change over the Internet. Working shoulder to shoulder and helping our clients understand their individual advantages and that of their department, division, or company is the way I prefer that IA functions.

In 2017, I listened to my team and we changed the name of our consulting operations group to IA Business Advisors. Still, this is only a DBA of Individual Advantages, LLC. For years, our clients referred to us as IA, and I appreciate the simplicity it offers our team and our clients. As I write this book in early 2018, individual advantages have been created for well over eighteen thousand clients in all fifty states and more than thirty-two foreign countries. While I have remained true to my philosophies of consulting, our organization has grown to a family of forty-two sister companies, all using the IA way, and all are viable and profitable.

Individual Advantages, as you can see, has been a journey for me, my family, and the people who have worked with me these past twenty-two years. Defining your individual advantages truly will be a journey for you. My goal is that you will take away from this book a plethora of individual advantages, the most important being that you are the single most important individual advantage in this world. It is through you that other individual advantages are created and realized by other individuals.

What Are Individual Advantages?

Well, each of us is individually a part of something that is itself, also, Individual. (Remember earlier when I discussed the use of lowercase *i* and capital *I* "individual"?) For example, a group of individuals create one Individual family; a group of individuals create one Individual country; a group of individuals create one Individual world. One individual is part of multiple Individuals; a child is part of one Individual family, but that child is also part of one Individual class at school.

As individuals, we each have our own, personal advantages, and through our own action we also create advantages for other individuals. Advantages are created by our influence over all that we interface with. Those we influence and those we are influenced by all create advantages for one another. When we work with other people, we become an Individual working toward achieving a singular goal. Each day is made up of interactions between and among many individuals and Individuals, and it is this choreographed task of communication and decision that creates the individual advantages that propel us in life. We are about to identify, in this book, how to better understand your own individual advantages, in every variation, and how those advantages create their own unique set of opportunities and advantages for other individuals. Advantages are the result of who we are; our actions and what we say have influence over all our interactions.

So, if advantages are born out of us, either individually or collectively as an Individual, what are they? Are advantages something we can use physically? Yes. Like being tall or strong. Are advantages something we can trade? Yes. You can barter, in a way, your own advantages to receive advantages that others have in return. If you are very tall and someone shorter than you needs help reaching something, you are able to use your height advantage to help that person. This act of kindness may propel the other individual to share their own advantages with you or with others. Kindness is an individual advantage; being kind to others can help build other advantages for the individual giving and receiving the act of kindness.

Are advantages an emotion, verb, or noun? Failure can be an advantage. Failure is something we learn from, and it teaches us lessons about whatever caused the failure and what comes next. Failure creates opportunities, which are advantages to be "taken advantage of." Happiness is an advantage over sadness. Action is an advantage over inaction. Decision to act on something is an advantage over being indecisive. The advantages we create are all these things and more. Advantages have the ability to propel us forward in life, but they also have the ability to hold us back when we do not choose to act upon them when they are presented to us as opportunities.

Think of advantages as capital to be used with other individuals. Some people are born into money; their advantage is that they do not worry about how to pay for things like education or material items. These individuals may appear to have more advantages than a child who is born into a poor family. However, the lives of these *seemingly* advantaged and disadvantaged people are not necessarily defined by the advantage of money.

Money can be an advantage just as lack of money can be an advantage; however, not all advantages are identified by a monetary value.

Affluent children may face challenges such as drugs or envy. They may grow up to be pretentious or sheltered from certain things that would give them more advantages or take away from their advantage. They may feel the need to keep their affluence and make decisions that will destroy them emotionally or, at some point, physically. Poor children, while lacking money, may have the advantages of a family or community that teaches children the values that brought them into this world. They may learn how to be more resourceful because of this lack of money. They may also learn how to need, through hunger or other physical challenges. These challenges will create advantages for them, such as the inspiration and drive to become something more. They may yearn for an education, instead of taking it for granted. That yearning is their advantage, and it is the advantage they will pass on to those they influence. Most advantages—empathy, patience, friendship, opportunity, education, and maturity, to name a few—come from within and are far more valuable than money.

We are going to explore your own individual advantages and how you can use them in the most positive way possible to hold influence in your own life and in the lives of others. Quite literally, everything we say, do, create, think, feel, and pass on to others becomes an advantage for you and those you influence.

We will begin this process through self-reflection—being honest with oneself. Identification of the individual we have total control over will lead us to understand our ability to influence our collective Individuals that we interact with daily. The influence we have will determine our ability to be successful within the areas where we choose to be active. This book will help you define your individual advantages, the influence you have over other Individuals, and the advantages you bring to them.

Opportunities vs. Advantages

How many times have we looked back at our life an hour, week, month, or even years later and said to ourselves, "I shoulda, coulda, woulda . . . ." First of all, if you didn't do it then, it was not time for you, and had you done it, most, if not all, of the great things in your current life may not exist today. For example, I believe I could have played professional baseball. I am certain that had I applied myself, I too, like a classmate, would have been drafted to the MLB to play baseball. Sounds great, but then I would not have learned the lessons I did, and this book would not be written in the context it is today. I would not have my three amazing children or my loving wife, René. Wishing that you did something in the past is destructive thinking. Life is a journey of many roads and many seasons; opportunities are life's way of giving us the lessons we need to reach the places we were intended to be at a certain moment in time. How often have you been presented with an opportunity that repeats itself, but you took it days, weeks, or months later? The lessons and goals you reached were a sort of destiny.

Opportunities confront us almost every day. An opportunity is really a chance to do something. To best describe what opportunity is, let's use the sales analogy. Pretend you are a car salesperson, and a couple walks in ready to buy a car; that couple offers you an opportunity to sell them a car. Another analogy: When you enroll in school and you read the list of classes that you can choose from; you have an opportunity to choose your educational path.

Opportunities can become advantages; opportunities are advantages that should be "taken advantage of." Advantages, by themselves, are created by our influence over all that we interact with. I once had an opportunity to make a presentation to a very large hospital in Denver, Colorado. My company was competing for a large Medical Information Systems integration project that would require a lot of technical and organizational change scope work. The chief information officer (CIO) of the hospital decided it would be a good idea to interview the four remaining competing companies as a group.

We all knew that we were going to be having this group interview, but we did not know who we would be competing against. My company had been working with this hospital for a couple of years, but our involvement was limited to single issues that were reactive, not proactive. This project was a long-term strategic initiative that would require resources and even more technical and organizational skill than our currently provided reactive consulting services.

When I walked into the hospital, I immediately knew I was the underdog. My firm was by far the smallest of the group, one-third to one-tenth the size of the companies we were competing against. I knew each one of them very well.

The opportunity of the interview changed when I was afforded the advantage of going last. The advantage of going last is what turned this opportunity into an advantage. We all had a stellar record of achievement when it came to the scope of work we were being asked to perform. As I sat there listening, I knew that at the end of the meeting I would need to make myself an orange in a basket full of apples; I needed to use my advantage of going last.

My opportunity to present my company began with the same background discussion everyone else used. I could see the eyes of the client's team begin to glaze over as I droned on about why my company should be chosen. At that point, one of the client's team members came right out and said to me, "Brian, your company is smaller than the operating divisions of your competitors. Why should we choose your team over theirs?"

Advantage is a funny thing, and using your advantages properly is often an opportunity in and of itself. That one question from the client established how to use my advantage of going last effectively. I looked at the questioner and then at my competitors, all of whom I had met and competed against time and time again, and answered, "Because my team has trained every person on their team how to do this project. So do you want the students, or do you want the teachers?"

You see, we had a training center that trained consultants from around the world. We had a tag line at the time: Our Trainers Consult and Our Consultants Train. To work for our company as a consultant meant that you also worked for us as a trainer, and we literally trained a good segment of the market in the services needed by this client.

The journey within this book will show you how to create individual opportunities, how to turn those opportunities into viable results for you and those you influence, and why having a complete understanding of the individual advantages that influence your life will help you and others to be better now and in the future.

We will identify how to realize the importance of the individual you influence or who influences you. Realization that, in all success, there is more than I. There is nobody on this earth who can claim that they are successful on their own, although we each play a key role in our own success. Some people call this being humble. I prefer to call it realization that in our own importance, that importance was created by other individuals with similar importance. There are still leaders and followers, primary roles and supporting roles. But each is important, and forgetting about those who got us to where we are in our journey devalues our individual advantage to ourselves and others.

Individual Advantages, as you will see, is about self. It is about image. It is about others. It is about influence. It is about prosperity. It is about acceptance. It is about structure. It is about accountability, and it is about teamwork. This book is the foundation of what I have been applying and teaching people for over twenty-two years. I have raised a family on these principles, a family secure in who they are and where they are in life. I have shared this way of life with my wife, René, for almost twenty-eight years. I have built more than fifty additional companies I personally owned and helped thousands of others with my original company, Individual Advantages.

2.0

Slow Down

"Wisely, and slow. They stumble that run fast." - William Shakespeare

To begin, we must slow down. There is no magic formula for slowing down; this requires willpower. The ability to slow down may be difficult, but one of the single most useful pieces of advice I give to people on a daily basis is to slow down. Slowing down is a cornerstone of the foundation of understanding you. If you are to look at what has made you who you are, you need to do so with patience, purpose, and an open mind.

Fast living manifests itself in many ways. Often, when we say a person is living fast, we mean that their life is out of control by way of risk taking. While it would be prudent for all of us to take stock of those parts of our lives where we may be living life too large (partying and other things we do that have potential harmful consequences), I am writing about a different type of slowing down.

I used to live my life like a bull in a china shop. I used to charge into projects headlong. I'm that guy who buys a do-it-yourself furniture project and throws the instructions to the side, thinking that I can build the piece by some kind of absorbed or intuitive knowledge passed on to me by my parents at birth. The speed at which I would get myself worked up was nothing less than amazing. As I began putting pieces together and finding myself more and more lost, my frustration and anger would be directed at that object because it was taking too long. Almost every time this would happen, René would say calmly, "Did you read the instructions?" Who has time for that!

I cannot tell you the number of times I spent twice as much time struggling with a project than I would have had I read the instructions and avoided my mistakes in the first place. I was the stereotypical man who wouldn't ask for directions. Even if we are in a hurry, we will drive in circles insisting we know how to get somewhere instead of stopping for a moment and asking for directions; thank God for GPS.

For me, the lessons in slowing down did not take root until late 1999. In April 1999, we moved into our new home in Colorado. This home was our first big purchase as a family; we built this home as a celebration of our success. This home would also prove to be a catalyst for me to go warp speed, as it required me to perform better as a professional and reach an imagined social status.

In October 1999, a friend and I stopped by the house during a work-day. Our intention was to have a cup of coffee before heading to a business meeting. As we talked in the kitchen, I went from cupboard to cupboard looking for the coffee cups—never finding them on my own. After about two or three cycles around the kitchen, I called to René in a very frustrated tone, "Where are the damn coffee cups?" The reply was classic René—with her blue eyes full of amusement and her freckled face, she opened the cupboard and did her best Vanna White as she showed me their very obvious place.

This story has lived on in our family as a humorous jab at my inability to slow down enough to locate the coffee cups in my own home after six months. But it serves as a great lesson about the lives of people who are always preoccupied with what comes next. We have a tendency to race through life to get to some imaginary checkpoint that is generally created by us alone.

Thinking Forward

Identifying the tendencies we have to go fast through life is the first step in slowing down. We are not like cars—just pump the brakes. Have you ever heard someone say, "Whoa, pump the brakes and slow down a little"? I wish it were that simple. I know I could easily do that to my kids who came running up in a fervor of emotion and with a jumble of words to express to me some immediate crisis they were faced with that demanded my immediate and very fast attention. My first comment, as my son or daughter tugged at my hand or sleeve attempting to drag me to the scene of the crisis, was always, **"Slow down."**

The most humorous part of this series of events is that I would say this to my children and then return to my own fast-paced thought process, where my mind was already two steps ahead of my previous thought, or better yet, find that I could not remember what I was doing, and I would turn instead to some other immediate need.

The coffee cup was not to be my defining moment; I did not learn from my mistake. In fact, it's not even the most interesting example I have of me going too fast. The event that defines going too fast for me as professional, and that I use day in and day out as an example, is what I like to call Peanut Butter Syndrome.

This story illustrates how the mind can take over when we are going too fast. The irony is not lost on me that peanut butter is in the story, a food that inherently slows you down with its gooey goodness.

One morning, I was in my typical rush (this won't be the last time you hear about my morning rushes!), and I was preparing for a big day to meet with one of our clients in the south side of Denver. This client was our largest at the time, and the project was very high profile. We were designing an order entry system for a manufacturing company with offices located in three states. The project included not only computer programming work but also business process re-engineering, as we were to integrate the system into the company ERP (Enterprise Resource Planning) and accounting systems for real-time data access from anywhere in the company. This was, and is, a typical issue for me as a professional, and like every other morning I already had the client on my mind. I was thinking about things I would be doing in three or four hours, things our team would be doing at that same time, and what we would be doing over the next three or four days, weeks, and months.

In my rush, I just wanted some peanut butter toast and coffee; easy enough, right? By this time, I actually remembered where the coffee cups were, but for the life of me I could not find the peanut butter. We had this food cupboard that went from the floor to about six-feet high—like a small pantry, which we called "Little Safeway." I stood in front of this cupboard with my mind racing about some flow chart, or a conversation at the forefront of my mind and peanut butter wishes someplace in the back. My frustration at not finding the peanut butter and the distraction from my important thoughts of factories and data had me once again calling out to René to come and rescue me from my own mind. This time there was no Vanna White moment. It was more like a flash of red hair and long arms reaching over my shoulder to grab the jar of peanut butter staring me in the face. With a chuckle and snort about my frustration at not seeing something right in front of my face, René handed me the peanut butter.

How many peanut butter moments does it take before you realize the speed of your mind is in control of even the most simple and basic things you see or do, even something as simple as grabbing food from the cupboard? René made fun of the incident. The peanut butter moment replaced the coffee cup moment very quickly. But for me, this was a defining moment. It was a keen reminder of how life can be too fast and how we can lose sight of what is right in front of us.

You may be asking right now, "How do I actually slow down?" This is a very complex question because, like all things, it needs to be put into context. My peanut butter syndrome affected the speed at which I oper-ated within the confines of my own home; going too fast affects everyone differently and produces various snowflake moments—each has a differ-ent remedy.

To best answer this question, I tell my own stories and can give advice on what I have learned. In the context of being in your personal environ-ment (home, family, vacation, friends, etc.), I recommend that you begin to remove work-related issues from the time you spend here. For example, create a single space in your home where you are able to work, and don't allow yourself to be distracted anywhere else with work issues. This exer-cise itself will slow you down. When you remove work from your personal environments, you will see that your attention will be accentuated. I used to work in my bedroom, kitchen, family room, garage—basically anywhere I had my phone—but I have an office at home now. The new rule at home is no work from my phone, tablet, or any document anywhere in the house except my office. I don't even answer the phone now at home; if it rings, I will physically disconnect from the personal things I may be doing and walk into my office area to review my calls. Even this, I will only defer to set working hours.

There are exceptions to all things, but I urge you to not make excep-tions to any rule you establish until that rule has become a new habit. If you allow a call "just this once," it will lead to "just this second time," to complete abandonment of the goal. Just as I am sure of this, I am also sure that your engagement with those around you, previously affected by your disassociation from personal life in support of your fast-paced work life, will be positively affected.

I also mentioned some other personal areas that really do fall within the context of my peanut butter story. When with friends, put your phone away. If you have children, give them a special ringtone and keep your phone on but ignore any ring that is not from them. When on vacation, set aside specific times, if any, when you will address work issues. For me, I wake up in advance of René and the kids and log in to my email and get my work done before they wake up. A small sacrifice to have 100 percent engagement with my wife and kids on vacation. In support of these actions, establish expectations from your team, employer, clients, or anyone under your influence who may think they are more important than the time you are spending with family during a well-deserved vacation.

Oh, and I have heard this a thousand times: "It's easier said than done." Look, if you have people in your life who cannot live without your absence from a work environment for five to ten business days, you have allowed an unhealthy reliance on you in those who do not understand what your vacation means.

Today, I know where every coffee cup and all the peanut butter is in my home. I also know what my family is up to, and if I don't it's generally because they are caught up in their own fast-paced issues. Compartmentalization of your time and where you work has tremendous benefits.

Environmental Urgency

Environmental urgency doesn't solely exist at home, on your personal time. It can exist anywhere. You may even find that it is most prevalent in the workplace. While you work on the speed of your environment in your own home, it may be worthwhile to work on the speed of your environment at work, too, so that something as ludicrous as this does not happen to you.

Have you ever missed a meeting? Not, have you ever arrived late, or have you ever forgotten to call someone. I mean, have you utterly blown off a meeting with someone? I have.

I served as a professional witness for a client's legal case. The client had nothing to do with any other business IA was involved in; our entire engagement was just to write a report. This client also had a skill that I saw as advantageous for more than a few of our other clients. His expertise was as a connector, as we like to call it; he had developed relationships around the world and, therefore, could connect people. Due to the sensitivity of the issue I had in providing the report for this client's case, both this gentleman and I went above and beyond to ensure that should we have any discussions regarding other areas of business, it would not have a negative effect on this case or cause any other conflict of interest. Both of us had discussions with attorneys and our teams in an effort to prepare for the opportunity to meet.

On the day of our meeting, I was prepared. I was excited about the possibility of having an asset that could solve a long-standing issue that was facing us at IA. That morning, I met with a couple of my team members to go over my later meeting with this client; we were preparing our last-minute due diligence. My entire day was built around this meeting (knowing that the lunch spot we had decided on was thirty minutes from my office). Around 9:45 a.m., I was hit with a number of strenuous client issues. These issues seemed to be fueled by their inability to slow down.

As you can surmise, I worked right through my meeting time and well into the next hour. My phone was on silent, my email alerts were turned off, and my door was completely shut, allowing me to deeply focus on the work at hand. I was brought out of this deep thought by a knock at my door and one of my employees asking me, "Weren't you supposed to meet Mr. So-and-so for lunch today?"

It was an hour and ten minutes past my meeting time, meaning it was an hour and forty minutes past the time I was supposed to leave. My client, being a gracious and rather calm individual, coincidentally also spent the time at our proposed meeting point working on other projects. He did not notice that it was well past the original agreed-upon time.

Do I miss a lot of meetings? No. Am I late for meetings? Yes. The issue of going too fast almost always creates delays. The domino effect of missing this meeting with my client caused a month-long delay in manufacturing, operations, and other areas of business for us both. First, we both have busy schedules, not just locally but internationally. Setting aside time to meet was already difficult, and the discussions we needed to have required us to be face-to-face. The act of going too fast, and missing our original meeting, meant we missed opportunities to connect with the other parties.

These missed opportunities were originally caused by both of us going too fast and being distracted by other issues; even though each of us woke up that morning with specific goals related to each other and projecting those thoughts and goals into our morning routine, we still allowed the urgency of our environment to distract us. While some may say this is an exception or a personal character flaw, twenty-five years of working with professionals and support teams has showed me that this is the norm. Speed of action and speed of thought, in most work and life environments, causes mistakes that ultimately cause delays.

Earlier I noted that not all types of going too fast are the same and that each requires a different remediation. My goal is to give you tools for how to avoid each type of "going too fast" moment. When you are going too fast to the point where you completely forget something, miss a deadline, and so on, you are distracted by your immediate environmental urgencies. Our goal is to challenge, and ultimately to change, this bad habit.

First, when you have an important meeting or deadline, have someone (whether it be a friend, family, or team member) hold you accountable. Outside accountability will not only help you to slow down, but it will also serve as a reminder on those days that you are deeply embedded in other things. (Having someone hold you accountable will aid in slowing your life down altogether. It will help you create a habit and may combat some of the difficulties that face us all in slowing down.) Another benefit of allowing a third party be your accountability is that it will help you practice identifying your tasks specific to that day's work.

Having a third party aid in holding you accountable may seem like an unusual task, but for many of us using technology as a reminder does not work. We have become so used to the noise created by technology that using technology as our accountability often fails. However, having a third party (someone in your office, your spouse, a close friend) support you in a habit change that will benefit you for the rest of your life is not a lot to ask.

For me, I ask René to text me or call me to remind me of important personal things. This is my first line of defense and serves to add one extra mental marker. Over time, I have been able to rely on this tactic less because I have built up the habit of listening to my technological reminders. My ability to remember personal tasks that in the past I would often forget has improved significantly. This new habit has spread into other areas of my life, and I have been able to improve my memory altogether through the act of this one simple task.

When I am at work, I rely on my team or peers for this accountability. I am open with my team about my ability to recall information or stick to specific schedules. I work with them regularly to ensure that individually I stay on track and Individually we continue to progress.

This accountability oversight does not need to last forever. Some may say that this tactic will result in total reliance on others for accountability. However, that is actually the exception, not the rule. When you focus on a deficiency you have and work proactively to rectify that issue, you create a moment and habit of slowing down to create your own mental marker. What generally happens is that when you have something important coming up, you are able to remember it before your third party holds you accountable, thus creating a new and healthy habit.

The second trick I would recommend would be to NOT turn off your cell phone. Sometimes turning your cell phone off is helpful when you need to focus on one thing, but when you are planning such a big event, it may be helpful to keep your cell phone on in case anyone calls to remind you (accountability!). When you are able to get in the habit of listening to your phone for reminders, you can set those reminders and alarms on your phone. There are tons of reminder and alarm apps for your phone and computer that can aid in keeping you on track for your day. They are truly helpful when you are able to break the habit of ignoring them.

Subconscious Mode

Going too fast can also manifest itself in our personal lives. I have a few hobbies, none of which require my focus for a long time. For example: I collect stamps. At certain times, I will give specific focus to them and then put them away for years before I even think about them again. Similarly, I like coins, building models, puzzles, reading, knives, and video games. Like stamp collecting, I get into these hobbies for a while and then set them aside for a longer while.

I have liked knives since high school. My stepfather, Bill, raised me from age thirteen on. He was a hunter and had a pretty extensive knife collection. As I got older, I too became a hunter and liked knives. My son, Henry, also likes hunting and knives. (As you may know, many sons tend to want to be like their dad.) One day I was sitting in the garage with René and Henry, and I was messing with one of my knives. It happened to be one I inherited from Bill when he passed away. Henry, at the time, was about eight. I was managing IA globally and a couple of very high-profile investments in southern Oregon: a hotel and a family entertainment center. My mind was very much in "subconscious mode" (a.k.a. autopilot) as I whittled a stick and contemplated issues at all three entities. Henry wanted to whittle a stick, too, and brought me one he found in the yard with a request for me to show him in the only way an eight-year-old knows how: persistent begging.

Now, despite my own position on slowing down and my experience teaching the value of slowing down day in and day out, Henry was interrupting important thoughts about clients, hotel rooms, and families at our entertainment center. So, to appease my son and the importance of all those immediate things on my mind, I told Henry I would allow him to whittle. René was quick to point out how dangerous it might be for our eight-year-old boy to "play" with a knife; to which I replied in haste that I would teach him knife safety. "Don't worry, I'm his dad."

The next few moments would slow down the rest of the day and the following week. In my desire to get back to thinking about client problems and hotel and restaurant operations, I cut off the tip of my finger teaching Henry about knife safety.

Cutting off the tip of my finger is a dramatic lesson on going too fast, and while it's not typical of what going too fast can cause in our day-to-day lives, the scar on my finger is my own proverbial reminder to slow down. Most of us on a regular basis forget something, leave something unfinished, drop something, or complete tasks in haste because of our need to speed through to another quickly performed task, and so on.

Sometimes it takes extreme examples to get a point across and to remind yourself to slow down. Going too fast manifests itself differently in each of our lives, and I hope that I never cut off another part of my body to remind myself. Other issues can involve missing key requirements. René is always telling me to make a list. I travel extensively and have for many years. I get ready for each trip the night before I leave. I use a CPAP but otherwise I don't have any special toiletries for travel; I rely on memory to pack those last. Depending on how fast I am going that morning, even though I have been packing the same way for twenty-two years, I will often forget something. Once, I forgot my CPAP altogether and had to buy a new one when I landed.

If you find that you often forget silly little things, or even big things, this is a key indicator that you are going too fast. This can manifest itself in other ways as well: Maybe you left things behind at work and had to backtrack; maybe you forgot something in your car; maybe you missed calls or appointments; maybe you lost track of time or words during conversations (possibly losing track of an entire conversation).

When speaking too fast, you may find that your audience cannot keep up with this fast pace; they may not be able to directly follow your train of thought. If you find that you must repeat yourself often, the reason may not be that they can't hear you or aren't listening. More likely, you are going too fast. When speaking, we often don't consider that the person we are speaking to does not have the foundation of knowledge of the topic being discussed. We as humans make this mistake often; we know what is in our head and what we want to say, but it doesn't always come out as clearly as we understand it.

As humans, we can quickly digress in our own heads, taking turns in conversation without warning others; these turns are the speed with which we think, which manifests itself in the lack of speed with which our mouths and audience can react. Digression is often a key sign of going too fast; it's the speed of our mind manifested in our communication.

In writing, you see this same type of issue. When you perform this type of going too fast it will manifest itself in what can only be called gibberish—in handwriting more so than in typing. When writing, we may quickly lose track of what we have written due to the lack of interaction with others—writing is a solely personal discussion. Our mind continues to speed along to the point that we can get lost in our thoughts—subconsciously typing or writing along—and only in our mind do we know the full story. However, you may find that the words don't quite make sense to anyone else.

I cannot tell you how many times a team member has handed back a paper of mine and said, "What are you trying to say here?" when I understand it perfectly in my mind. Originally, I hand-wrote a good portion of this book in my Moleskin. The variation in my handwriting is bizarre; I must have close to ten different styles with one hand alone—and I'm ambidextrous. This is a clear manifestation of how fast my mind is going and what kind of headspace I am in while writing. Conversation and interaction can slow the process down. With my team, I have to keep in mind that no one else has the context of the issues I am trying to write about.

Going too fast can manifest itself anytime and anywhere; when it does, the best advice I have is to slow down. You will see improvements quickly and find that you are more efficient. Being able to benefit from the act of slowing down will take time and patience with yourself. If you are like most people I have encountered, you may even have some push-back to the act of slowing down.

What can be gained by slowing down and not rushing through tasks? You may say to yourself, "There is no way I can go any slower, there is not enough time in the day!" My initial reply is always the same: We all have the same amount of time in a day. The conversation always leads to the amount of work that "needs" to be completed in that same amount of time.

We can always come up with an excuse to not slow down. Our boss has demands. Customers have demands. Peers have demands. How about you, do you have demands? Self-reflection can be a big part of slowing down. Is ego causing you to push past your limits? Do you have an image of yourself and your work that propels you to move quickly, impressing others with your hard work and drive? What would happen if you slowed down to 90 percent of the pace you are at? What about 80 percent or even 70 percent? What situational awareness would you develop? How much more focus would you have? How much clearer would your own internal and external communication become?

Immediate Gratification

Speed can result in miscommunication and negative communication. Time demands and the internal need to speed along can put nerves on edge and create environments where people tend to communicate less or in ways that are ineffective. We find ourselves reacting to another person's haste or impatience with negative judgements, often steering the discussion onto tangents that only feed the negativity and provide nothing constructive to the original issue. Going too fast tests patience, and in today's world of need for immediate gratification—or I should say, of our demands for information or action—a lack of patience often leads to disagreement.

I still struggle to find solutions to the need for immediate gratification. We are bombarded with a need to immediately react or complete tasks—sometimes consciously but more often subconsciously. One only has to walk down a street full of people to notice what today's technology has done to humans' need for speed: immediate gratification.

When I travel, there is one universal action that is consistent in every town I visit: cell phone usage. Cell phones are no longer just a phone; they are phones, TVs, work, computers, game consoles, and much more. Want to freak out a human between the ages of thirteen and fifty? Take away their cell phone.

With applications available to us, we can manage most of our life on our cell phone—from communicating with people to turning on the lights in our home. Want to know where your teenager is? Look it up on your phone. Missing your favorite TV show and don't want to wait? Get the Hopper™ by Dish and watch on your phone in real time.

These kinds of technologies have created the immediate need for gratification. Patience is waning in all aspects of human interaction; impatience is being felt throughout the whole of society. I identified this issue in my dissertation long before it became a common human problem: Technology Induced Attention Deficit Disorder (TIADD).

There are many places in society where this manifests itself on a regular basis. Let's begin with a prosaic example of immediate versus lasting gratification: Cupcakes.

To eat a cupcake is to have immediate gratification. Most people enjoy cupcakes like Lay's Potato Chips: you can't eat just one. Those who eat cupcakes in search of immediate gratification of their need for sweets may be jeopardizing their potential long-term gratification of being fit and healthy. Individuals focusing on how they feel now often lose sight of the long-term consequences of a single, but repetitive, act. Occasionally eating just one cupcake is not bad, but eating several cupcakes has derailed many plans for a thin summer physique.

The Internet is another place where humans have adapted to expect faster gratification. In 1995, when I began using the Internet on a regular basis, I used AOL as my service provider. My first modem was a 14,400 baud rate modem that made crazy digital sounds and required me to use a phone line to connect. I would sit in front of my computer and wait patiently for it to download messages, photos, and website content, amazed at the amount of information I could access and work with on my computer.

In 1997, when I was designing ERP (Enterprise Resource Planning) systems around the world, I began working with 128,000 baud rate digital network connections that did not require a standard phone line. In two years, the speed at which we communicated over the Internet had increased tenfold. The amount of data we could transfer and share also increased, allowing more people to access this data and allowing us to do more. The wait for messages, photos, and website content decreased tremendously.

By 2001, when I argued my dissertation about TIADD, I was still designing and implementing ERP systems and working with companies to manage the organizational change being caused by technology's effect on humans. Internet access rates were increasing, and you could get a 128,000 baud rate at home and 1,544,000 baud rate at work. In less than five years we had again increased the speed of communication over tenfold. Humans quickly adapted to this increase and raised expectations for their data.

Through the years, from 2001 to now, we have seen data speeds increase more than fiftyfold. We have also expanded the influence of technology from the workplace, to home, to the back of your pocket. This transformation in data delivery has created an insistent need for immediate gratification of knowledge; we need answers this instant.

This need for immediate gratification has had a negative effect on human relationships in all aspects of human interaction: from quality to quantity. In 1997, if we wanted the immediate gratification of speaking to a family member/friend/lover, we picked up the phone, wrote a letter, or visited them personally. We took our time and the conversations were thoughtful and memorable. How many visits or phone calls to people in your life do you remember?

Christmas of 1990, I had just begun dating René. I already knew I was in love with her, and our first months of dating had been typical of the time; we talked on the phone and saw each other as often as we could. René and I had had some "missed communications" already, which had made me kind of insecure. So, while shopping for René at Aurora Mall in Colorado, I stopped at a pay phone and called her. That call lasted for almost an hour, and to this day is something we both remember. That hour-long phone call had meaning; it had context.

Today, we text. We talk about life and what is going on in life, but I cannot tell you anything meaningful that we discuss via text. Unlike that phone call almost twenty-eight years ago, texting is immediate and at such a speed that most of its content is lost as soon as we are interrupted with the next text, email, or other notification—it has less meaning in the grand scheme of our life.

There was a lot of long-term gratification in communication prior to the advances in communication technology. Today, people post tweets or make a Facebook post and immediately satisfy that need to say something to remain relevant. Almost gone are the days when we cut out a news article about a loved one or put a picture in a photo album to create a book where you sit around the table and look at those things that once provided long-term gratification.

The propensity to quickly move from issue to issue and juggle texts from work, friends, and family, while we are also trying to perform manual tasks at work or home, diminishes the value of the information we receive. In our workplace, we often see gaps in work or mistakes caused by the interruptions that come from the amount of information being thrown at us. I am guilty of this myself and sometimes to the detriment of my team. Brenda, who works with me on a daily basis, is seated right outside of my office. She is responsible for work that requires great focus and detail; I know this, as does she. However, I often just yell out to her and interrupt whatever she is doing to satisfy my own immediate need. If I'm not in my office and want a similar response, I text her and skip email—knowing that she will respond more quickly to a text.

My need for immediate gratification may resolve the issue at hand, but it instills in me and those I influence the habit of allowing interruption to invade our current chosen task. These interruptions create risks that either my work or the work of the person I am interrupting will not be completed to the best of our abilities.

Focus requires us to find a way to keep ourselves and our influence in sync for our personal and team objectives. The best way to do this is to create a deliberate environment.

Deliberate Acts of Focus

There is but one overarching way to slow down, and it's called being deliberate. Being deliberate requires discipline and focus, but once you develop the habit of deliberate action, the world around you will slow down to a pace where focus becomes your first by-product. There is always a way to be deliberate in all we do. I will use face-to-face communication as my example here.

When speaking to someone, either one-on-one or in a group, how many times do you allow for distraction? I'm not sure any of us can be involved in a conversation nowadays without distraction from cell phones. One of the rules implemented at IA is that cell phones are not allowed out in the open when dealing with a client. It is imperative that each member of our team become deliberate with the time they give to our clients. Too often we will be communicating with someone and they will look down at their phone, distracting themselves, undermining the integrity of our discussion.

Not allowing yourself to be distracted by a phone is a deliberate act of focus on the conversation you are having. This is not a hard deliberate act to begin with, and it will slow you down and refocus your attention on the matter at hand: the conversation.

The second deliberate act you can have during in-person communication is to look at the person speaking. Physically looking at the person speaking will help you to focus on what the person is saying, and not daydream or digress in your own mind about some other task or issue that is not currently relevant. Looking someone in the eye conveys something to those you are communicating with and in turn to you: respect. One of the first compliments I get about my children is that they look people in the eye when speaking to them; my children have learned to focus on those who speak and to show their respect. This kind of respect will earn you the same in return.

The acts of paying attention by removing distraction and of looking at those who are speaking will slow down the rate at which your mind accepts the communication you are collecting. Your mind is not trying to listen to one person across the room and at the same time read a text message or email from someone else, where you then must focus on a reply, emotion, or feeling you now have from the information you are reading. Pretty soon you have missed a sentence, paragraph, or more from the person speaking. This is a common issue with multi-tasking, the ultimate form of going too fast. When you slow down your mind's processing of information, you become more efficient and more of a positive influence in those areas where you have it.

Comfortable Focus

Another type of going too fast is what I like to call "comfortable focus." This is the state in which we become so accustomed to what we are doing that we no longer think about the act of what we do and just go through the motions. Comfortable focus is being so comfortable with what we do that our mind wanders while our subconscious and physical self complete tasks. (Other terms for this are "autopilot" and "muscle memory.") Some may see this as a form of multi-tasking; I see it as allowing the world to pass by, along with opportunity and advantage.

The best analogy I have for this involves driving. Driving is one area of our lives where we can often go too fast. I'm not necessarily talking about how fast we drive, but how many thoughts we have and the things we do when we drive. When we moved to Oregon and then later to Illinois, I had relatively short commutes to my offices: two miles in Oregon and eight miles in Illinois. The path to the office, in both cases, was pretty simple; not a lot of turns and stops, meaning that I could get into a routine and drive the route with a comfortable focus. One day while driving to work in Oregon, I looked up and saw a house I had never noticed. This, after three months of the same daily drive. Why did I notice that house after three months? I had to slow down due to construction and actually pay attention to what I was doing.

Going through the motions and being comfortable with our surroundings or people can lull us into a false sense of security. The National Highway Traffic Safety Administration reports that approximately 52 percent of all accidents occur within a five-mile radius of home, and 69 percent of all car accidents occur within a ten-mile radius from home. This false sense of security leads people to think that talking on their cell phones, eating, and getting lost in their music while driving is safe since they have a muscle memory for the roads. While knowing the roads closest to your home is appropriate, you also need to be prepared for the child who darts into the street chasing after a ball or the reckless driver who is also in a comfortable focus and may not see you.

Getting into our cars is a form of emotional and psychological comfort and security. Most of us feel comfortable enough to not think about the action of driving. However, that feeling can stretch beyond the drive. The more we repeat something, the more of a habit it becomes, and we begin to take for granted the time we have during these actions. It is during this time that we can speed up our minds and allow ourselves to be subconsciously arrogant about our ability to complete certain tasks. You may be saying to yourself, "Driving to work and not recognizing a building or sign has no real effect on my life." While this may generally be true, the process of comfortable focus can get to a point where important things get missed, as this next story of my atypical morning will reveal.

My mornings are generally as structured as my drive; I am typically in a comfortable focus for most of it. The only thing that varies is the clothes I wear; "to wear a suit or to not wear a suit" is the constant variable in my morning routine. This particular day I had to wear a suit; it was not an ordinary day. I rushed to get ready for work as my mind was overly occupied with a meeting I was about to have at a big hospital on the south side of Denver. This meeting was going to be different; my company was being considered to be the hospital's consulting partner in the development of a new medical records management system, and we were the new kids on the playground. Needless to say, I was playing out my presentation in my mind.

It was an early summer morning, so René and the kids were still asleep. I put on my sport jacket, slipped on my wingtip shoes, and double tied them as I always do. I blew through coffee and breakfast, which was not typical of me at this time in my life; I typically enjoyed my mornings at home. We lived on a golf course and our backyard was adjacent to the fifth tee box; we also had a lake and another whole fairway for hole four behind us, not to mention a complete, unobstructed view of the flatirons and Rocky Mountains. But, on this day, the striking view was lost on me because my brain was thinking forward.

However, when preparing for work I know how I prepare best. I don't really procrastinate in the sense that I put things off subconsciously. I put things off to a point where the demand to get them done gives me added focus and drive; now who's fooling who, right? Comfortable focus helps me here in the mornings. I don't really need to think about getting dressed, making coffee, driving to work; I could do most of that in my sleep.

With my mind racing at full speed, the act of preparing my physical self was in comfortable focus. (By the way, I am also a car guy.) It was a nice day out, a little cool as Colorado mornings can be, but otherwise a beautiful summer morning. Our home in Colorado had a tandem three-car garage, meaning that on this day I was going to have to move one car to get to my car of choice: my 1997 Porsche 993 convertible. With my mind still focused on work—skipping from bullet point to bullet point about the solution we were recommending to the team of professionals I was going to assign to work with the hospital and our plan to be better than companies a hundred times our size and eons older—I went through the routine of moving cars and putting the top down on my car.

Ready to leave, I made one last round of checks in my home, which I still do today. I look to make sure I have put my coffee cup in the sink. I say goodbye to everyone in my home, even guests; this habit is so ingrained that to have closure on my morning, I won't miss a single person. I will look over my tools of the trade, my briefcase or computer bag, to ensure that I have everything I need for the day. I rarely forget anything at home.

Being ready, I hopped into my car now sitting outside in front of the garage. We lived in a quiet area north of Denver with little early-morning traffic. As I pulled onto I-25 South, I got a chance to put my car through some high-rev acceleration and quickly got up to seventy to eighty miles per hour, all while keeping my mind focused on work.

It would not be until close to I-76 (about thirteen miles into my drive), where the highway becomes congested and there are a lot of feeder highways onto I-25, that my mind would snap out of its comfortable focus of work and onto the road. This day, however, I noticed more of a breeze and the fact that I had indeed missed something that I could not give my presentation without: my pants.

Somehow, I had managed to get through my entire morning of comfortable focus with no pants. My habits were so ingrained and automatic that I even double tied my shoes with bare legs.

Our minds can do things that defy simple logic. Noticing whether or not I had pants on should be pretty logical. Putting on my suit coat, tie, and shoes should have been enough for my mind to notice something this obvious. Walking around, getting in and out of cars as I move them, and leaving one outside running while I put one back to then go back into the house to do my goodbyes and check for all my tools of the trade—you'd think I'd recognize even the slightest difference. But my comfortable focus with my routine of the day, coupled with my speed of thought, was powerful enough to allow me to not only prepare for my day without noticing, but to drive thirteen miles down the highway until my focus was broken by the one thing that could slow my mind down enough to notice: traffic.

I began consciously thinking about living in the present about the same time I drove off with no pants. In fact, the drive back to my house was accomplished without noticing anything other than the thoughts in my mind about how I could have walked out the door without pants.

Living in the Present

I realized that I needed to be present to understand 100 percent of what was happening. Living in the present is a form of slowing down. I immediately equated traffic on the highway with the issue that caused me to walk out the door without pants; traffic makes you come back to reality, back to the present. Traffic forces you to focus on the cars in front you and to both sides, even behind you. Traffic makes you slow down and pay attention.

Being present is a conscious effort. The trap of comfortable focus can overtake us before we know it, until something snaps us out of our trance. Being present is something that we can learn just like learning to walk, and for many of us it will be just as difficult.

In the morning, I set myself up to be present throughout my day. I create reminders and alarms on my phone and notifications on my Outlook calendar; luckily, these simple tools are available to us all. Over time, I have developed the habit of listening to these tools to break my comfortable focus and bring me back to the present. Being in tune with our chosen methods of remembering things requires some work and the action/habit of listening to your reminders. There have been countless times where I have slept through or worked through my reminders; I had to train myself to react and to develop the habit of reacting to these tools. One word of caution: Do not allow yourself to ignore these tools or the act of ignoring them will become part of your comfortable focus and they will be ineffective.

The mind itself is such a powerful tool. We can use our brain's power to our advantage; we only need to work the parts that will support our desire to be in the present. The two things we need to train our minds to acknowledge our outside triggers—or, I should say, to not lock us into such a deep focus that our mind takes us from thought to thought and action to action while in comfortable focus—are habit and willpower.

Later in this book, I expand upon habit and willpower and the influence they both have on our ability to be the best for ourselves and others. Our own influence on others is affected, and can be limited, by our habits and willpower.

This brings me to disruption, because breaking your comfortable focus will often feel like a disruption and evoke negative emotions within you. The second piece of effectively getting into the present is controlling those emotions. Being a person who gets so focused on work to the point where one is almost in a trance means that unexpected distractions can be quite upsetting. Each distraction brings us back to the present, which often means away from the one of many places we were in our minds. This is where data can be lost too.

I often find myself in my office working on tasks only to recognize that my mind is wandering to other areas of responsibility before that set-aside time. I may be waiting for a call, have unfinished tasks from the past, or have learned some new information about a project. These distractions from my present task are easy for me to control now; I write them down on a pad of paper. Calling them out and putting them to paper slows down my mind enough to get me back to the task at hand.

However, there are times when an interruption will make me lose track of the work I was trying to get done. At that moment, I may stop everything in an attempt to get my bearings back and stare at my desk while my mind restores the right visuals in my head. These distractions raise the emotional frustration I feel. The emotion is led by two issues, one being that I cannot believe that I cannot remember what I was thinking about twenty seconds prior, and two being that I am not happy with the person who interrupted me or the reason I was interrupted.

I have created some rules in support of keeping me in the present. (I help to hold myself accountable!) One is that I have shared with everyone in our office that walking in and distracting me when I am obviously focused on a task could elicit a brief negative response as I transition from my comfortable focus back to the present moment and their needs. If I really need to focus, meaning that I need deep-mind-work time where my present moment is intended to be comfortable focus on a specific topic, I close my door and turn off my phones. I also ask people to notify me if I think particular work may take me into that trance state.

Living in the present is not about being available to all the chaos around you. It's about understanding your current situation or having situation awareness and controlling your present focus. I'm not saying that comfortable focus is not needed at times; we all need time to lose ourselves in our own mind, work, or hobby. But we need something that can bring us back to overall present awareness and allow us to function without missing life as it goes by.

The things I do to keep one foot in the present include setting up distractions in my environment that can bring me back from my focus and force me to take note of the present: task reminders, visual cues within the documents I am working on, Post-it® Notes, or (as I have mentioned previously) having a peer interrupt me at a specific time. These planned distractions can serve as a breather and will allow you to check preplanned schedules, agendas, or other organizational tracking tools to ensure that you are meeting your own timelines for the tasks you want to complete.

One note about implementing planned distractions: You will find that if you previously reacted poorly to a distraction, you will continue to do so—at first. The habits of going into deep concentration and losing track of time, then coming out of that in a foul mood, are two separate issues. While I don't generally like working on multiple habits so closely connected, these two require some collaboration. Be honest up front about your reactions and consciously remind yourself internally or with other visual cues, as we have discussed, that becoming present is a goal; for example, one of the cues I put up is, "Don't get angry with disruption!" This cue and others are on Post-it® Notes around my office, workbooks, and computers to remind me to be nice.

Intention

One of the best ways to slow down is to become intentional in all we do. To be intentional, we need to be focused. And to be focused, we need to slow down. One cannot be consistently intentional unless we set our intention. If it is your intention to have patience, what must you do *today* to aid in achieving that patience? Does this include meditation? Time alone? What actions will you take to accomplish your intention?

The difference between a goal and an intention is that goals can feel abstract, while intention is linked more directly with the actions needed to reach goals. The abstraction of goals stems from the fact that goals are rooted in the future, while your intentions are focused on the present moment. Your goals have a concrete end and beginning, while your intentions should be lived out each and every day. Lastly, the steps by which you achieve your goals can be seen and measured by others. Your intentions are personal, so they are part of your internal self-communication.

Deceleration of your fast-paced life can begin with the process of setting your daily intention. For me, I carve out fifteen to thirty minutes of my morning and set my intention for the day. This action of setting aside the time was in fact an act of intention to reach my ultimate goal of slowing down my entire life. Through the initial act of looking at my day ahead, I reinforce a number of intentions in my life.

Here are some intentions that are affected by my initial act of setting my daily intention:

Overall Intentions

1. Make sure that I am living to my fullest potential for all those I influence and that I am the most important person in my life.

2. Take responsibility for my personal self, reflect on overall goals, and remind myself to remain present and slow down.

3. Remember that others influence me and that their influence is part of why I am successful.

4. Be prepared for my day and have a clear understanding of my scheduled responsibilities for that day.

5. Remain educated and relevant in industries I influence through my coaching, advising, and consulting.

6. Reinforce my team by understanding any issues they are facing and asking for support on.

These are high-level intentions that I have set for myself. I feel that these six intentions lay for me the foundation to succeed personally and professionally. I also believe that these intentions, when read daily, create in me the ability to remain present and slow down enough to ensure that my influence over my life and others is objective, clear, and with proper intention. I have paraphrased my intentions and reinforce them visually by writing them in my daily planner. "Remain Educated and Relevant," is a common scribble. "Be Prepared for Your Day," is another.

Each morning I read what I call "trade rags." My use of trade rags, or trade magazines, blogs, and newsletters, is a way I have remained educated and relevant for years. I advise my clients to utilize them to stay up-to-date on what is going on. One can garner vast knowledge from industry publications that you would not learn in five years of operations. People who share their experience and knowledge through print compound our knowledge and make us more intuitive in the areas we learn about.

My intention to read about my areas of influence is fueled by my passion to be the best I can be as a consultant, leader, peer, and person. Connecting your personal goals to your intentions will help to reinforce the goals and make the intentions more available to your present self. Without some motivation behind intention, the action of being intentional can be lost in the chaos and clutter of your life. Your intention to change, learn, act, speak, or listen can be missed and then lost. Intentions are the seeds of action, similar in this way to goals.

When we are intentional, we immediately slow ourselves down. The mere act of setting your intention provides for you the focus that you need to achieve those intentions. When you do this, you should get in the habit of limiting outside interference: email, text, people, and so on. My recommendation is that you do this in a closed, private room. You may find that during this intentional moment, other thoughts will pop into your head that are not meant to be thought about at this time. Keep close at hand a paper and pen so that you may write these thoughts down and refocus your attention on your intentions. For example, I often find myself working on a project when something triggers my mind about some other issues I may need to deal with. When this happens, I sometimes pivot to that new issue and lose focus on my current one; I lose my intention. My office is littered with the notes I write to myself during these times.

Whatever way you choose to keep your focus, you must make time to be intentional about your thoughts; have a separate time to focus on your new notes and turn them into something you can act upon. It boils down to this: You must become intentional about managing your intentions. For some, this will be a simple task; for others, it will require practice.

Setting your intention should be something that you strive to make a habit. Creating habits in support of action that will slow you down and keep you focused on all that you influence will be some of the best personal work you can do. Later in this book, we will look at how to reinforce your personal goals and amplify your ability to be successful in your quest to meet those goals.

Slowing down also encompasses overall time management. Setting your time for being intentional will not work if you don't gain control over all of the time in your life. Developing habits that reinforce positive intention is good, but let's look at time from a different perspective.

Time Flies By So Quickly

Does it have to? When I hear parents say, "Wow, kids grow up fast," I can't help but think, "Really? A day is a day. You must have been distracted by life." Each of us has one challenge that is shared by every individual: time. Time is always moving at the same speed, in one direction. What changes is not time, but only the perception of that time. What we as humans do with this gift is our biggest advantage; what do you do with your time?

Time has not always been measured as it is today. Until the nineteenth century, time was basically relative; there were no standard time zones adjusted by location on Earth. By this I mean that the current time differed from city to city; in one city it could be 12:40 p.m., but in the next city it might be 1:20 p.m. according to the town clock tower. In England 1883, however, railroads were becoming more popular. The trains were relied on to move people and material from places through England, and the relative time of each city was becoming an issue. England decided to standardize time based on the meridians of the world. In 1884, the adaptation of time zones began to catch on, and now we have standard time zones around the world.

What do time zones have to do with time flying by? Perception. Soon after the development of synchronized time, the world began to look at time differently. We began to measure time against productivity and other variables that can be affected by time. However, some of the things we never measure with time are tasks that are beneficial to us individually. What we have created today is a lifestyle based on tasks that are often managed and measured by time. What happens next is that time becomes our focus in life, and time takes over.

When we allow life to take over and don't slow down to "stop and smell the roses" on a regular basis, we end up with a whole life full of time-flying-by moments. The mind can often wander off from what is happening presently and onto what is coming next. The problem with this type of going too fast is that it can have a long-term negative effect on us.

Humans today tend to measure success by the amount of time put into something, not on the quality of what that something is. I often hear the words "I've put my time in." I hear people want to be measured by the time they worked someplace or the time they spent on some task. People will use time to measure almost all things associated with actions such as work, working out, and sports. What we don't see is people using time to organize individual tasks like time with family, recreation, education, or most other functions.

It is this common habit of ignoring personal time that I think makes us humans feel as if time has flown by. I also believe that if we would pay attention to that one moment that is most critical to us as humans, the present moment, we would all slow down and begin to take control of time in our own lives.

"Live in the present; the most important moment in your life is the present moment. It is in the present that all things are learned, lost, and forgotten." I wrote this back in the summer of 2017 when this book was just a twinkle of an idea in my mind, and to this day I often forget to stay focused on the present. Despite all my efforts to create in my life a habit of staying present, I find myself digressing to thoughts of the future and the past on a regular basis. You will find this happens to you as well. Training ourselves to live in the present moment is not an easy feat, but by acknowledging that we don't live in the present, we have already taken the first step toward being present.

Not living in the present moment and permitting our brains to be elsewhere—thinking—creates gaps in our memory where we have lost focus of our surroundings and have not fully absorbed what has happened. Training the mind to slow down and focus on our surroundings is not an easy task. You have to want it, to actively try to obtain it. Realize what is going on around you. What did you eat yesterday? What conversations did you have? What emotions did you feel? What parts of life did you actively participate in and take notice of? To realize your potential individual advantages, and those you are creating for others, you must slow down and see life now.

Getting to the point where you can answer some of these questions, regularly, will take some willpower. Willpower is the ability to hold yourself accountable for your internal goals. It is that inner voice that urges you into action or inaction. Slowing your life down will require willpower.

Willpower is finite, but it is also individual to each of us. Teams can have collective willpower that can carry their members through together; this is called collaboration or teamwork. Each of us can use our willpower to move ourselves and others forward. We will spend more time learning about willpower in Chapter Five; keep in mind that to live in the present, and be focused on the now, you will need to use willpower.

This development of living in the present will become a journey that lasts the rest of your life. Your ability to capture the present will come in fits and starts. Like any new habit, you will find yourself "off the reservation" and back to taking time and yourself for granted. Living in the present requires you to accept that this happens often and will happen for the rest of your life. However, the more you practice time management that works for your life, the better you will become and the more you will see that living in the present slows life down; your memories and quality of life will be better.

There is a lot of debate on whether quality of life today is better than it was in the past. To many people, better is a subjective concept that can only be measured individually. When people tell me my life is better than their own, I remind myself that the statement is made out of ignorance and out of context; they have no idea what my life is other than what they see on the surface.

Is my life better today than, let's say, the life of my grandfather? Or maybe the life of my ancestors in the 1500s? Do you ever see in history books the question, "Are people happier now than they were then?"? These questions are explored in Yuval Noah Harari's book *Sapiens: A Brief History of Humankind,* and they make me reflect on the present and how we approach the present.

This perception of a better life is what many people strive for, but it takes away from living in the present. Humans today, especially Americans, often worry about what others' perceptions are of their individual. The quest to appear visually in control of our life by living in certain homes, driving certain cars, or dressing in certain clothes creates the need to live a life that is out of control with regard to time and often much more.

The ego that drives this quest robs us of our ability to enjoy the present moment and focus on the myriad of tasks we try to cram into our lives to reach the heights we strive for that give people the perception that our life is better. What I'm here to tell you is that if you gain control of the time in your life by living in the present, you can actually create for yourself, and all those you influence, a better life.

You cannot regain time. Your past is your past. One second ago is now a part of who you are. Every second that goes by is another moment to achieve your dreams, to become who you want to be, to positively influence another person or yourself. You can do so much with your time—with your life. Do not waste it mindlessly elsewhere while your body is here just going through the motions. Do not wake up in one, five, or even fifty years and wonder where your life has gone because your mind has been so lost in comfortable focus that you forgot to take the time to live. Living in the present moment is the art and act of slowing down. When *now* becomes a deliberate piece of your life, your life becomes clearer. Now is the time to gain control.

There are a number of ways to get in the now, the present moment. The first step is recognition of the time in your life you remember the least about; I'm talking about your current life. For me, I often sit down with a pen and paper (or on my computer) and just write out my last few days—like a list.

A typical Monday to Friday for me at home looks like this:

6:00 a.m. Woke Up

6:05 a.m. Made Coffee

6:10 a.m. Wrote in Journal

6:30 a.m. Made René Tea or Coffee

6:45 a.m. Chatted with René

7:05 a.m. Looked at Trade Rag Articles on
    Phone or Played a Game

7:30 a.m. Left for Gym or Work (Gym not so much)

Gym Time: Listened to music as I got through my workout

Office Time: This is where I lose track.

In fact, most days I cannot tell you what I have done after I arrive at work. This issue has persisted for as long as I can remember. I know that I proactively slow myself down at work numerous times throughout the day, but unless I review my working timeline where I log my hours for clients, I could not tell you what I do. What can really hurt you at this phase of your life is what many people think is an asset: Multi-Tasking.

The Turbo Charge of Going Too Fast

My advice on multi-tasking is: Don't do it. Ever.

The negative effect of going too fast can be compounded by multi-tasking, another form of going too fast. We multi-task to get more done in the same amount of time. Multi-taskers are often celebrated for their ability to do so many tasks at once, but at what cost? The American Psychological Association states, "Doing more than one task at a time, especially more than one complex task, takes a toll on productivity."[1] We use contrasting parts of our brains to complete different tasks. When one part of our brain is focused on one specific task, the other parts of our brain are, essentially, muted. When we switch between tasks, this forces our brain to "jump start" other areas of the brain for use. This reduces productivity and increases the amount of time needed to complete a task, because it takes our brain time to switch gears and access the knowledge stored in the different areas. Similarly, we cannot use our brain's power to give an equal amount of intense focus to several different tasks all at once.

1 (2006) Multitasking: Switching costs. In: American Psychological Association. http://www.apa.org/research/action/multitask.aspx. Accessed 22 Feb 2018

Focusing on multiple things at a time diminishes our ability to access all of our stored knowledge for each specific task, thus, in turn, reducing productivity and diminishing the quality of the final product.

Multi-tasking is synonymous with lying or stealing when it comes to work. *Stay with me here.* You're not really giving your full effort to that one task. Think about this: If you are paying for someone's time, and that person's attention strays to anything else during that time, would you receive a discount? If a plumber comes to your home and the job takes two hours of his time, one and a half hours spent working and the other thirty minutes spent answering phone calls or talking to you about the weather, would you receive a discount? What about the workers who text all day long, spending twenty seconds here and twenty seconds there?

Pew Research Center conducted a study in which 1,035 participants were surveyed over the course of ten or more study breaks. The study found that 97 percent of these smartphone owners used their phone to text during their designated study period. While this study was not at all surprising to us, as many people do use their phones at work, at school, and mostly at home, it does show that people naturally take time to answer texts/IMs/emails on their phone while they are clocked in for work.

A good way to combat the turbo charge of going too fast is to plan out your day in advance. Set aside a few minutes in the morning (or the night before) to look over the tasks you have at hand for the day. Think about these questions while doing so: How many tasks do you NEED to finish by the end of your day today? How long will each of your tasks take to complete? What is the priority and importance of each of your tasks? Which tasks will require the most brain power? By answering these few questions, you will then be able to plan out your day accordingly and will steer clear of multi-tasking (making you more productive!).

Prioritize the tasks of most importance to be at the beginning of your day. The tasks that require the most brain power and that are due that day, or have a close due date, should be the tasks you do first thing in the morning. Next, do the tasks that have a medium amount of importance but require a good amount of brain power. You will want to schedule all your hardest and most challenging tasks closer to the beginning of your day and save easy, brainless tasks (like replying to emails) for the end of your day. This type of prioritizing will help keep you on task and will aid in productivity.

If it works for you, you can also try breaking up your day into segments once you have your task list for the day complete. Some people like to break their days up into thirty-minute increments, with one- to two-minute breaks in between to reset their brains. Others like to plow through the task and then take a short ten-minute break to give their brain a moment to switch gears to their next designated task. The important thing to remember is to give yourself small and short brain breaks to ward off exhaustion.

Find what works for you. During your brain breaks, we recommend moving around a little bit. Even if it's just a quick walk around the office to fill up your water bottle, keeping the blood moving in your body will help your brain tremendously. And while these short breaks may seem counterproductive, you will make up for this time with the added productivity you have by focusing on one task and avoiding multi-tasking.

It is imperative that you take note that every situation has an exception. We state this regularly as the situations we discuss are common, but there is always an exception to the rule. When you work in a position that doesn't allow you to focus on one specific task at a time, you need to have the capacity to work efficiently in that setting. You need to know that your specific job does not allow you to single-task. For example, as a receptionist you may need to be interrupted frequently and quickly switch between tasks as the phone rings or as people come in to speak with you. This is inevitable in this kind of position, but the people who work productively in positions such as these are unique in their ability to resume the task they were working on prior to the interruption. They are able to plan for these disruptions and schedule their work accordingly.

It is also important to note that distractions will happen. When you are focusing on just one task you may be disrupted. The point of not multi-tasking is to not plan to do multiple things at once, to do your best to focus on the one task in front of you, and to understand that you may become distracted by things that are not in your control.

The Workplace

There is a gentleman in the office where I work who, I swear, is always going a thousand miles per hour. When he walks through the office, he looks like he is practicing to race walk in the 2020 Olympics. His hair is usually disheveled, and when you talk to him he speaks hundreds of words per minute. Those of us who are in tune with him know that there is one way to slow him down; speak with him about fishing.

The transformation in him when we bring up fishing is amazing. His speech slows down, his body language changes, and he seems to regain some clarity in his life. The conversation will seemingly go into slow motion because now we must endure his recap of some fishing story, and getting him out of this happy place can be difficult. But, he will slow down, and that will remain his new pace for the next hour or so—until his tunnel vision returns, and you see him fly by again, off to the races.

Our habit of speeding through life can carry over and affect us at work. Going too fast can become cyclical, causing us and those we influence to speed up our lives in all aspects. Work speed can have a dramatic effect on us and those we influence in mostly negative ways.

Speed at work serves to reduce overall quality, as sloppy work is poor work. Speed in the workplace is only a requirement in professions where being speedy is essential; for example, for first response teams or medical personnel reacting to an accident or other medical emergency. However, for those of us who are in sales, management, and services, going fast does not lend itself to quality in any fashion.

This is where I often get pushback from clients: "What? You want me to slow down my staff?" Yes. I will ask, "What is so important that if staff took 15 percent longer to do that task, the company would be negatively affected?" I want to be clear here: Speed and focus are not synonymous. When we previously gave you the tools to focus more efficiently on each task at hand, that did not mean to speed through each task. It means to focus on each task. Speed sacrifices quality.

Let's look at work environments that often demand speed and where quality suffers:

Fast food service is an industry where speed is essential and where we accept a reduction in quality of product and service. The price of these products is such that procedure is the foundation of quality; if people follow procedure, then quality will follow. However, the demands of speed often override the advantages of procedure, and quality often suffers. How many times have you been to a fast food restaurant and found too much of one ingredient on your food? The cause of this is speed. How many times have you opened the bag to see your food discombobulated in the packaging? The reason is how fast the food was prepared. The demands to get the food out are flashing above the young high school student on a screen screaming, "Go faster or the customer will be unhappy!" but the speed of action will itself make the customer unhappy.

Professional services are another industry that often demands speed. Legal, accounting, engineering, and management firms measure utilization as one of the key performance indicators (KPI). However, demands on timelines for clients often push the envelope of what we humans are capable of. Then, we begin to rely on multi-tasking and co-mingling our mind power with action—often doing two, three, or four projects simultaneously. The effect of this is missed tasks, inaccurate work product, and scope creep (digression from the main objectives) due to the re-work or additional resources needed to meet our obligations.

Sales are a process. Some people are lucky enough to be in a field where the sales process is simple; the customer may come to the salesperson, and all that is needed is help setting up the delivery process for what is being purchased. Other sales require a lot more detail and often persuasion; this process can take hours, days, weeks, even months. In all sales, there is an urgency on the part of the salesperson and perhaps on the customer as well. In the reactive sales process, the customer may rush through the process of buying an item or service, and due to this speed of action, they may not get what they really wanted. In that same situation, the salesperson, knowing that the sale will be quick and realizing that the customer is pressed to make a purchase, will often not ask questions that would clarify add-ons, changes, or other opportunities; the goal is to move past this sale on to the next. In the long sales cycle, frustration in the process can lead to shortcuts, inadvertent misrepresentation—often caused by the speed of the sale—and lack of communication and understanding. Regardless of the result, the common denominator is speed of action.

Speed of action can actually result in delays, whereby if we had just slowed down in the first place, we would have actually taken less time. A good example of this is if the customer or salesperson rushes through the ordering process and makes an error that results in sending the wrong item. The result of this is that it will take longer for the correct product to reach its destination, and the tasks needed to fulfill the order will have been done twice to rectify the issue of going too fast the first time.

Another example is my son Henry. We will be getting ready to go someplace and he will wait until the very last minute to get himself ready, resulting in him forgetting something that forces him to return home and take up twice as much time than if he had just slowed down. I do this at work if I'm rushing to a meeting; I forget things like my phone, cards, and notebooks.

Speed of action and decision can affect almost all career fields. Here are some common issues we see during projects:

Construction

We have seen project managers skip over critical tasks, such as following up on closing out tasks that are prerequisites to future tasks, because of a propensity to multi-task. The ripple effect here is that people don't realize they can begin the next task in sequence, and when they do, everyone goes too fast as the project manager pressures the team to make up for deficiencies in the schedule. This increase in pressure and continued reliance on multi-tasking generally compounds the problems.

Project managers can also make assumptions regarding tasks and direct their tradesmen to complete tasks out of sequence or prior to other tasks being complete. This generally leads to work being re-done. This method is costly in time, material, and labor and leads to present and future delays. An example of this may be a project manager who directs the drywall contractor to close some walls; however, due to this haste, the plumber or electrician may still have work to do inside the wall, meaning now the wall must be reopened and then closed again, furthering delays and cost overruns.

Finally, safety can be compromised throughout the jobsite. Some workers may skip wearing eye protection or other personal protective equipment (PPE). Jobsite evaluations may be missed in an effort to "get to work" quickly, thus missing a key issue and leading to a safety event.

Architecture/Engineering

We once had an issue with a hotel property we were building. The architect used the wrong measurements on one part of the blueprints. This issue compounded with other issues as it was only on one side of the building. As the construction team began its job, they noticed the foundation was two inches too short. This caused massive delays in the project as they scrambled to fix all the calculations.

These types of issues are often caused by procrastination on the part of the professionals, who then find themselves facing deadlines and rushing through calculations and documentation. These issues can be intensified as the data is passed onto another who may have similar traits and demands, creating problems that if found early on during the process may have been less pervasive. However, due to the demands often associated in certain careers, they end up becoming more pervasive and even dangerous or costly.

Medical

Medical professionals are famously pressed for time, and in some cases the urgency is needed. We've all heard stories about medical instruments being left in a patient (this is a classic issue of going too fast). However, many times medical offices will try to see too many patients by overbooking themselves. We've all had to wait in a doctor's office past our appointment time, another by-product of trying to do too much.

I address this issue often; I have even written about it. You arrive at a doctor's office for your appointment. You wait five to as many as sixty minutes past your appointment time. I have had opportunities to track the staff's work attitudes throughout the day with some of our clients and at my own doctor's office. The day begins on time. The staff then begins to feel the pressure of time as they usually begin with thoughtful communication and care. As the pressure mounts and the delays grow from five to ten minutes and then to twenty minutes, the staff becomes stressed as well as the patients.

I know that my blood pressure has been elevated and recorded due to the stress of delay at the doctor's office. I also know that the delays at my appointment create my own need to speed up and go faster, leading to my own issues in my profession.

I could provide examples for every single profession I have consulted to, but that would result in the writing of its own book. I am personally guilty of many of these examples and often excuse my behavior and the results. Regardless of who has caused the delay, I have to own the delay and the effect it has on my life and those that I influence. I can either tackle the issue head on and risk speeding up or utilize my team to overcome the urge to speed. Together we are able to refocus our time, expectations, and performance in support of our goals of being deliberate. Our proactive instead of reactive approach allows us to have a firm control of our immediate future.

S.M.A.R.T.

One of the best management tools for speed of action that I like to share with my clients is the S.M.A.R.T. (Specific, Measurable, Attainable, Realistic, Timely) process.

Specific

A lack of specificity while communicating can produce outcomes that are not intended. The people we communicate with do not have the privilege of reading our minds. The context by which we communicate is only known to ourselves, so we must communicate with specific details until our point is 100 percent understood by the other party. Specificity is a trait that will require you to slow down in order to achieve what you want in an accurate manner the first time.

Non-specificity creates confusion and can be very costly. It can lead to digression from the task (which is a time loss), inefficiency, and conflict. Consequences of non-specificity can range from fixable to catastrophic. I have known people to omit all negatives (consequences) from scope documents. A full understanding of the consequences in any document is vital for reaching the true goal. Specificity in all things is how you remain on the same page with all parties. Being specific will reduce the likelihood of scope creep (digression from the main objectives).

We once were contracted to develop an order management system for a large metal-building manufacturer. The system appeared to be pretty simple—this was back in 1999, prior to the complexity and tools we now have available in technology. This system was to be tied into the company's ERP system, which would take over the data management process of managing the design, manufacturing, packaging, delivery, and finalization of payment. The company had dealers around the country and wanted them to use a uniform order entry system that supported the business processes.

We had been supporting this client for a long time, and I had designed its ERP system. I spent many weeks at the client's factories around the United States, working side-by-side with their teams during the ERP development. I decided it would be best to hire an outside contractor to provide the computer programming to create this order entry system. However, due to my intimate understanding of the client's business, I wrote the scope documents for the programmer in verbiage that was quite vague.

My frustration with the programmers began when they did not seem to grasp the concepts of what we were doing. My response to the persistent questioning was to tell them to go the company's offices and ask for clarification. So, they went to the office, specifically to one of the new salespeople, and asked them what they would like to see in the program. This led to other conversations with individuals who knew nothing about what we were trying to accomplish.

By not being specific about the scope, I had created an opening for errors. By not being specific about whom to talk to, I created an opening for scope creep. We ended up losing about six weeks of work. The issue was my fault because I had not been specific. In not being specific and not paying attention, I allowed for this project to digress. We eventually learned from our error and got the project back on track.

Being specific does not end with task description; it includes all aspects. Review clarity of message with anyone you delegate a task to or to whom you pass on critical information. Know that by not being specific, context or details will get lost in communication. It's good practice to end these types of discussions with, "Do you understand …?" and having them repeat back to you what it is they understand. If you are an individual who has been given a task and you do not understand, ask for clarification.

Finally, try to remember that people cannot read our mind. What's in our own head and what we are trying to convey in conversation is clear to us, but those receiving the information may lack the context we have. Being specific is about providing that context for people so they understand what we are trying to communicate. You can achieve this by slowing down, using simpler words, getting to the point, and not digressing during conversations that involve conveyance of important information.

Measurable

If you cannot measure it, you cannot control it. The act of measuring is another deliberate act that supports slowing down. To measure you need to be specific, and to be specific you need to slow down. Create a way by which you can measure progress. KPIs (Key Performance Indicators) are measurements that will force you to identify progress; it is a proactive action if done regularly. When you set up a way to measure, you will slow yourself and the process down, ensuring that you are being proactive about identifying where you are in relation to your goal.

It's also very important to know what needs to be measured. Almost everything we do personally or professionally can be measured, but we often measure incorrectly. How do you choose a proper KPI? Well, that depends on your goal and is unique to you based on your position toward achieving that goal.

I'm going to use a personal issue that many are measuring today: steps. If the ultimate goal is to lose weight, then measuring steps is only one KPI that should be focused on. If we reach our 10,000-step daily goal, but eat 3,500 calories and don't measure that, we defeat our step goal. Our KPIs should include measuring calories and steps in order to achieve the ultimate goal of losing weight. Other KPIs that can be measured to achieve this goal are fat, protein, carb, or sugar intake.

Since we know what our goal is and what our limitations are, we can better plan our lives and schedules around these KPIs. Measuring for yourself will be difficult. We cheat ourselves and are our own worst support system when tasked with holding ourselves accountable. We can form all manner of excuse and justification for cheating ourselves. When developing measurement, ensure that you include some form of accountability.

Attainable

Your goals must be attainable with the resources you have. If you don't have the resources and you set the goal, shortcuts (speed) will result in a product or service that does not measure up to your goal (unless your goal is to accept substandard results). Many people and organizations set unattainable goals. They do not take the time to understand what is needed; they speed through the process of goal setting, which ultimately creates unattainable goals. Ensure that what you desire is attainable. If you are specific in what you want and can measure the progress, you likely have an attainable goal.

Some of the aspects of goal setting that are often unattainable are time, funding, support, and ROI (Return on Investment). For example, we often hear our clients ask for projects to be completed in a timeframe that is not conducive with what we are working with. On the surface, these requests suffer from a lack of specificity. For example, a client may say, "I'd like to develop product X and have it to market in six months." Product X may be something they have already prepared for submission to vendors that can produce it, but at what cost? The client may have a limited budget, further making attainment more difficult. Then they may choose a price point that requires manufacturing be done in China or some other foreign country.

Each demand on its own may seem attainable. Can we make product X in six months: yes. Can we bring product X to market on budget: yes. Can we sell product X at the price point the market is dictating: yes. Can we do them all at the same time: no. When you have separate demands that are attainable on their own but not together, you will have to adjust some of the demands until they are all attainable. This is where being specific comes into play. Within the details of specificity, we keep our tasks attainable.

Realistic

If you're not realistic, your goals will not be attainable. We need to ask ourselves, Can I reach this goal with what I have available to me? Have you been specific with what you need? Can you measure progress and keep track of the effort and assets needed? Have you determined that what you want is attainable with your resources? Being realistic is difficult. Often, the reality of a situation is that we cannot do what we want.

There is a common issue in business that is caused by being unrealistic. I can honestly say that I address this issue with as many as twenty business owners a year and speak about this unrealism in one form or another during most of my presentations. I call this issue bandwidth.

Most of us think of bandwidth as the capacity of data through a network; I use the term loosely to describe the capacity of just about anything. Business owners often think about one thing: sales. They push for sales above all other aspects of the business, and then bandwidth gets in the way. Sales are important, but if owners and managers focus on sales without also focusing on the company's ability to fulfill sales (bandwidth), there will be issues. When owners do this, they create other issues that further affect their ability to reach maximum efficiency. If owners align their sales bandwidth with their operational bandwidth (which is supported by the organization's administrative bandwidth), we have parity—or what I like to call operational integrity—which will lead to maximized profits and success.

We once had a client who was an amazing carpenter. He worked strictly in office buildings and one day decided that he would start his own construction company. He leveraged his relationship with building managers into work. He then needed to hire some people to support him: laborers, project coordination, and office administration to begin. He began with $200,000 in capital and was a natural salesperson. He quickly filled out his schedule but saw right away that he would run out of money, so he hired a project manager to sell more jobs and help him manage his current one. Growth means more money, right? Wrong.

His company grew into being owed hundreds of thousands of dollars and having no available cash. He could not pay his employees or vendors. The stress caused him to project his frustrations on everyone he influenced. His drive to grow sales put him in a position that could cause bankruptcy, though he was flush with sales. Growing your business beyond your ability to service those sales will result in failures in your ability to perform the service, to collect for that service, and to address any issues that come up during that service. Any of these issues can kill a company.

Another area where being unrealistic is pervasive is in the expectation to resolve problems. Most people we deal with face problem resolution in a totally reactive manner, so they only address the most visible aspect of the issue. Most individuals don't dive deeper to find the root cause. Without determining the root cause and rectifying the true issue, you create an unrealistic perception that the problem is solved.

As leaders, we often pressure our team to solve the most immediate issue and move on, not really giving support to the team to dig deeper. The expectation that we can lead in this manner and be effective is unrealistic. Eventually, the root cause issue will result in a bigger failure.

One of the most common effects of this is loss of team members. Not empowering people with the time and resources to deal with the root cause of issues wears people out. Failing to look at and find the root of an issue, and then setting a measurable and attainable goal for the team to resolve it, creates unrealistic expectations and demands on the team.

For example, say we have an employee who is constantly missing deadlines. We see that that employee's deadlines are being missed and only address that issue. Our solution may be to take away some of that employee's tasks and reassign them to someone else, who then begins to miss some deadlines. The reaction to this may once again be to move tasks to another person; re-creating the same issues. This may go on for a while, depending on the size of the company or the issues. Without actually looking at why the deadlines cannot be met, we never uncover the true issue.

We see this often in companies with distributed tasks, meaning that the company may rely on people to do multiple tasks, none of which are independently in support of the other required tasks. These people multitask through issues that are not connected, and the distraction of one is not in support of another. Further, the end results don't necessarily support any of the other tasks; leaving the person with a lack of support or connectivity. These people can be easily distracted and digress often from one task to another, never quite sure what is due when.

We can resolve these issues through business process reengineering or adding some simple task management tools. Other times, there may be a wholesale change in how the organization sets expectations for its employees or tasks. Setting realistic goals for employees means being specific, making them measurable, assuring they are attainable, and guaranteeing they are timely.

Timely

Time is the one thing that we never seem to control. For one, time never stops for anything or anyone. If there is one pressing issue at work, it's time. Is the market ready for your product or service? Have you established a proper timeline to reach your goals? Have you been specific about the time it takes to perform tasks, get information, or complete actions needed? Can you measure the time needed? Is the timeline attainable, or do you have the resources needed to be timely in your efforts? Is the timing realistic?

One of the companies that IA manages has eight patents. These patents are specific to EPA (Environmental Protection Administration), NFPA (National Fire Prevention Association), ANSI (American National Standards Institute), and IKECA (International Kitchen Exhaust Cleaning Association) standards, rules, and laws. It would be easy to assume that the products developed to resolve and meet these different organizational standards would be timely for the market, but that would be wrong.

Drive down a street full of restaurants. Look at the fans on the rooftops (most look like mushrooms) you may see a dark streak leading from the fan; that is grease. The discharge of this grease is an issue for property and personal safety, fire hazard, and ground water contamination. Look at the used grease dumpsters in the back of those same restaurants; you will notice a similar streak leading away—more of the same issues as on the roof. Patents and products to address these issues have been available to solution providers for the past thirty years, yet 85 percent of all restaurants are not in compliance.

Why is this issue not providing timely access to the manufacturers and service providers who resolve them? Accountability. While these rules and regulations are in place, most of the market is not being held accountable. The providers often create ad hoc solutions, not really designed to properly contain or support the containment of the issues.

A manufacturer who sees the problem and reads the rules may feel he is being timely; not in this case. Because the AHJ (Authorities Having Jurisdiction), such as the fire marshals, building code inspectors, and ground water managers, are not really looking at the root cause, the market is not demanding proper resolutions from the service providers. Thus, we have 85 percent noncompliance and no accountability; innovation in this space is lacking.

This example can be duplicated across countless issues facing us today. The answer to this is applying S.M.A.R.T. to our daily lives and tackling the root cause as an Individual team and using our influence properly.

Reaction

Another action that speed often interferes with is reaction. Emotions can interfere with our ability to create advantages in our decisions or actions. Reactive tendencies often eliminate opportunity by alienating us from people or opportunity that might otherwise provide an additional advantage to us. How many times have you overreacted to an issue and in doing so changed your life path?

Back in the mid-1990s, I sold my first company, Business Accounting Solutions. When I sold this company, I worked for a few additional companies as a contractor. During that time, I traveled a lot between San Francisco and Denver, and the expenses were quite high. As a contractor for companies, I billed for my time and expenses. One day I received a check that was for about half of what they owed me, which was unexpected. When I called, I was informed that there was a chance that I would not be paid any more funds. My reaction was purely emotional.

Having a direct relationship with the CEO of the company, I went down to their offices to meet with him and immediately took an emotional posture. I informed him how it should be and in so many words how it would be if he did not pay me the full amount. He informed me that the company had money issues, that the check in my hand was all he could promise and that it very likely represented the full amount of what they would ever pay. He also told me that they did not disagree with what was fully owed, but that this was a matter of his company's survival.

My reaction to his calm demeanor was to get angrier. I reacted to his ability to look me in the eye and tell me he was not going to pay me. During the time he was explaining his company's position, all I thought about was the money he was withholding from me. My mind was calculating the loss, and the loss was feeding my anger, and my anger was feeding my mouth with words that were unprofessional and quite frankly only hurting me.

My last action of the day with this client was to reach across his desk, grab a pen, and write VOID on the check he had given me. I threw his check at him and told him that he owed me the full amount and that I would collect my money some way. My client looked at me with almost humor, but I suspect from what I know today, it was pity. While he looked at me he calmly said, "Do what you feel is right for your company, I think our business here is finished."

I was so angry that I stormed out of the office, and my first call was to my attorney. During my call to the attorney, my emotions began to subside, and I reviewed the events that had transpired. My attorney calmly interrupted, "Did you keep the check they gave you?" My answer was only about halfway out of my mouth when it hit me; I had thrown away over $3,500.

That company closed shortly thereafter. Some other company got my money, and I got an expensive lesson in emotion. Later in this book, you will learn how the next reactive moment in my life would cost me millions of dollars and a friendship.

There is a moment after we have made a mistake, after the consequence has set in, where we look back and ask, "How did this happen?" only to realize that the information we could have used to avoid this issue was there all along. We were only going too fast to realize it then. What opportunities have you now missed because of this mistake? The act of slowing down, that initial act, can be one of the most amazing moments in the span of time. That first act of pause can give you an epiphany, the clarity of thought, for your "ah-ha" moment on the issue at hand. When you create a pause, that moment is one individual advantage that can be life changing. A pause can clarify for you a past issue, which can be used as a tool going forward and living in your present moment. How you create the pause and what you do with the pause will bring you back to the present moment. This present moment will give you the advantages you should have.

To begin, you must slow down; stand still long enough to look in the mirror and face the reality of your actions and where they come from. This is a cornerstone of your foundation, self-awareness, and acceptance. To realize your own individual advantages, and to learn all you can from your life experience and that of others, you must slow down. Take the time to find what it is that helps you slow down, whatever that might be. Talk about fishing, take a hot shower, play a video game, meditate, work out, cook, write, draw. Slow down to realize your full potential.

3.0

Who Am I?

"Our vision will become clear only when you can look into your own heart. Who looks outside, dreams; who looks inside, awakes." - Carl Jung

HAVE YOU EVER LOOKED INTO A MIRROR AND THOUGHT, "…Who am I?" One of the consequences of going too fast in our lives is that we lose track of who we are. When we begin to slow down, not only does our present life come into focus, our past life does as well. I can honestly say that up to the age of about thirty, I did not reflect on my childhood or where I came from. I did not sit and contemplate the effects of my past on who I was, other than maybe my education or work experience.

My childhood created a foundation for who I am today. That foundation includes many flaws and opportunities that have helped to change the direction of my life many times in my fifty-two years. My past is filled with joy, sorrow, regret, anticipation, love, and loss, emotions that add to the pragmatic experience of education and other unemotional life lessons. Even as I sit here and write this book, I am struck by the question, Who is Brian Smith? Maybe a better question is, Who do I want to be? Is it okay to ask that question at this stage in my life? Yes.

I'm going to digress on my original question above: Who is Brian Smith? Not too long ago, I was with a client whose team kept asking me, "Why do you want to help us?" (I get this question a lot.) This client is a large food manufacturing company that is almost a hundred years old and still in the same family. The company is amazing. The company has employees who have dedicated their working lives to it; this company was built on the backs of employees like this. When I answer this question with,

"It's what I like to do," that is not enough for many of the leaders at this company; they want a more complex answer.

I like what I do because I get to help people realize who they are and give them an opportunity to either accept this or make changes. When I work with people, they always get something from me, either validation of their current situation or information that leads to some new direction, even if I am not involved in that new direction. Many companies move on without me and our team and find a way to alter what they may have been doing. Other times, they just keep doing what they were doing.

One example is indicative of what we face as consultants. One day one of our team members introduced me to a new potential client. This man sat in my office and outlined his business issues (which were very negative). During the discussion, the client boasted about his math skills and the very complex spreadsheets he created to manage his business (which was failing). After the entire story had been outlined to my and the potential client's satisfaction, I told him we could help him but it would cost about $35,000. I told him I would provide a detailed project plan that would identify how we would help him and in what timeframe, and I asked for a $5,000 retainer.

The potential client made a choice to not use us and also to ignore some of the detrimental information shared during our two-hour meeting. Two months later, he was sitting in front of me with his primary shareholder asking me to go over the plan I had mentioned two months prior. However, circumstances had changed for him and his company. Two months prior, he had been in debt but not in default; now, he was in default with his creditors and could not pay his employees. It was four days before Christmas.

This man had thirty-seven employees, most of whom lived paycheck to paycheck. I knew that if I did not help him, all thirty-seven people and their families would be dramatically affected. I reiterated what I told him the first time but informed him that the price would go up. The reason:

Helping him now meant that we needed to get his staff paid and begin to effect change quickly. If left to his own devices, he would fail.

We came to an agreement, and the next day I walked into the client's office and handed each employee a paycheck three days before Christmas. The client stood next to me and explained that we wanted them to focus on their families for the holidays but to return to work afterward with renewed spirit. Together we would ensure that this would never happen again in this company.

Eight months later, all thirty-seven employees were still employed there. We sold that company to a larger one, ensuring that the business plan and people working toward its success were stable. Today that company is surpassing its objectives and has increased its workforce.

This is why I do what I do and try to find a way to influence people; I believe that I have an ability to help people realize their potential, individually and collectively.

The second question above: Who do I want to be? I am who I want to be! At work I am the guy who helps individuals find who they are and realize that they can be whoever they want to be within the context of their effort and abilities. To be the person that you want to be, at work or at home, you have to understand yourself on all levels. To understand yourself to this degree means that you understand, or at least recognize, that you have an inner and an outer you.

My experience has shown me that there are basically two of each of us; one is who we are on the inside, and the other is who we are on the surface. Now, I don't mean this in a purposefully fake way, I mean this generally in a healthy way. People are not always what you see during your interactions. We are all made up of our experiences, good and bad. Our past has influence on who we are, yet you cannot wear all of that on your sleeve all the time. For example, how many times have you experienced something that you knew was just ridiculous? Sometimes when the event is so ludicrous, many of us will accidentally blurt out what we have just witnessed and then immediately think, "Did I say that out loud?"

This is a glimpse of the inner self. Generally, this is the part of us we like to keep inside or at least reserved for those who are, in our minds, safe to share that part of our self with. There is then the outer you. This is the person most people know you to be. Often, there is a great divide between what we portray in our day-to-day life versus what is really inside. Some of this dissension can be found on the surface.

I used to fly to Illinois once a month from Oregon. I did this from September 2010 to June 2013, when we moved to Illinois permanently. During my trips, I had the opportunity to meet with two men who graduated from the high school I attended in ninth grade. The circumstances of this meeting were that my client in Illinois had grown up with these men and at one time had been their partner. My client is a fairly grounded person; he is to a certain extent fiscally responsible. As I sat and listened to his former partners brag about their assets, I remembered some data I had recently seen about these two, specifically about the extent of their debt.

About halfway through the lunch, one of the partners looked at my client and said, "Is that a Timex watch?" My client, looking down at this watch, just answered with a simple yes. The former partner quickly produced his watch: a beautiful Swiss timepiece and confided that he had just purchased it for $160,000. My reply was so immediate it even shocked me: "Maybe that's why you're millions of dollars in debt."

Now, I don't begrudge people spending their money on nice things. I am a capitalist and believe in the free market. However, pretentiousness for the sake of self-fulfillment in the face of self-deprecating actions and stupid assertions make me crazy. By this, I mean there are people out there who risk security for themselves and their families to fulfill a need to be pretentious. Like in my example above, spending $160,000 on a watch is something done for self-fulfillment. On a less grand scale, people may buy cars, homes, or clothes in support of similar needs but to the detriment of their financial or emotional well-being. More than a few times I have witnessed people celebrate paying retail, and each time I wonder how they like paying the highest price for something.

Understanding oneself begins with one often forgotten fact: We all have an ego. Understanding that this is something wholly human is our first step to understanding the complexity of what ego does to the question, Who am I?

Ego

What is ego? Ego is purely human. It goes beyond instinctual actions. Ego drives our personality, action, communication, and perceptions. Ego can be complimentary or damaging.

Ego is your sense of identity, and it can help and hinder you. Ego is your self-esteem or, for some, your self-worth. Perception can play a huge factor in what you or others perceive as your ego. Behind a camera, many may become shy or come to life, while off camera, they may feel the opposite—lively or introverted. Different contexts reveal different facets of our ego.

Our ego is driven by many factors. It can be driven by your physical stature: good looking, fit, or put together. Ego can be driven by your education, income level, or social crowd. Ego can be influenced by yourself or by others. Ego is something that can be propped up in a flash and then dashed (taken away) just as quickly. Ego can feel good to some, but the perception of that ego can make others feel bad.

We used to have an associate who has an amazingly large ego. This associate is what some would typically call a "pretty human." Good looks, well spoken, and generally above-average intelligence. If you worked with this person, you would be impressed by his organizational image; his look is clean and tidy. In fact, this person would describe themselves as having "the Clark Kent Look."

However, wherever this person goes is left a path of wonderment: how can someone with such talent and opportunity allow his inner self to emotionally and physically conflict with his outer self? He is the perfect example of the struggle between the inner and outer self. On the outside, he gives the impression of neat and tidy, yet he is highly disorganized and dirty.

I once got into his car, and it was absolutely filthy. Not cluttered; filthy. When I brought this to his attention, the excuse was that it was an old car and no one was ever in it. A week later, however, I saw him with his kids in that car. That image stayed with me. Intermingled with that impression was memories of the associate's poor interactions with others. Those interactions usually indicated that he had no issue with his massive outer ego.

Fast forward to when the associate bought his dream car. About a month after the car was purchased, we had an opportunity to ride together on the way to a client; I let him drive. This new luxury car was spotless on the outside, but as soon as I opened the door it was pure filth—again. It was dusty, dirty, and messy. It smelled of sweat, dirt, and fast food.

The contrast between the car outside and the car inside was much like the contrast embodied by this person. On the outside was this superficial exterior that looked good and sounded good; on the inside was chaos. On that same drive, he immediately put on what I can only call "gangster rap" and began to drive aggressively. Now, I don't care what kind of music anyone listens to. I myself have a very eclectic playlist that includes artists such as Eminem, Katy Perry, Disturbed, Foo Fighters, and Mozart. I am also no Sunday driver. I enjoy my cars and tend to lean on the more aggressive side of driving.

However, the volume of the music was turned up after we began driving. I don't know, but maybe when you're driving with your direct superior on the way to see a client, you don't immediately turn up Wiz Khalifa. However, I wish it stopped there; we took off like we were rushing to a fire.

I turned down the radio on my own: "Really? Rap at full volume?" The reaction I got to my words was a look of incredulousness; like, how dare you touch my car or tell me what to listen to. This all occurred as we sped away from our office at seventy miles per hour in a thirty-five miles per hour zone.

I made a comment about his driving and received the same incredulous look. While our drive continued, I began to inquire as to why his brand-new dream car was so dirty and why he drove so poorly; the non-answer and look of confusion as to why I would even ask answered my question. The final kicker was our turn toward the client: a high school business incubator team. (The high school that my son attends has a team of kids each year that create their own potential companies. We help them with the logistics of the business, and at the end of the program they pitch to a "shark team" and are awarded money for their ideas.) We were in a school zone, and as we blasted through that zone at sixty miles per hour, I could not help but feel empathy for this person and his ego.

This story may have you wondering, What could this possibly have to do with who I am? Your inner self or subconscious can manifest itself in strange ways. For this person, his ego manifested itself in a dirty car and erratic driving. When confronted, he had an excuse for every action or lack of action; the dirty car was a result of a lack of time and the driving was a result of me being an old "fuddy-duddy." In reality, he thought only about himself.

What we need to remember is that what's inside influences what's outside. Many of us protect the outside from our inside; what we think is not what we say. When we allow ego to commingle with our external self, the risk of showing those parts of us that we don't want the general public to know about goes way up.

If you really want to grow, then you need to face your own demons. You need to reconcile how others see you, how you want others to see you, and who you want to be when you are alone. During this reconciliation process, you may not like what you see; it may scare the living bejesus out of you. But if your goal is to be someone who you are not today, then you must go through the entire process to be that person. If you find that living one way and being another is exhausting or creating chaos in your life, begin with being honest about the contradictions you live with.

To see yourself clearly in the mirror, you must become humble. One of the best ways to learn about yourself is to ask others. Stop, slow down, and gain situational awareness of yourself in your most common places. Stop and look at where you sleep, where you shower, where you eat, and where you drive. Stop and look around your workplace. Ask your peers, especially those who rely on you for something, What traits do you see in me that I might want to work on?

Have you ever been called selfish? If you have, you may want to ask yourself why. Instead of quick reactive justification, seek to ask what could label you as selfish. Have you ever been called arrogant? Again, why would someone call you this? Do you justify your arrogance under the guise that you're just that good? Does being "that good" mean that you should exhibit arrogance as a by-product of being good?

Do you react in anger to things that don't go your own way? Why? Is your ego so large that you feel that anger is the only way to communicate your displeasure? Does anger deliver your message better than empathy? I used to wear the badge of being labeled an asshole like it was some medal of honor. My justification (ego) said that I could do this as long as I was honest about my "asshole" actions. Really? There is no human on earth who has earned the right to treat another human being poorly; that is just not something we should be proud of.

Another ego-driven trait is impatience. I have been guilty of this. Knowing what I know and at times expecting others to know what I know does not give me the right to flex my ego in the form of impatience. Impatience is one of the ego-driven issues that can cause us to make others speed up, and we have clearly outlined what speeding up can do to us.

Ego drives more bad decisions than it does good ones. However, our ego is not all bad. Ego also provides us with a means to keep moving forward. One of the best examples there is of ego gone right, and wrong, is sports.

In professional baseball, the best hitters can fail more than two-thirds of their times at bat. Good hitters have batting averages in the range of .300 to .350. As children, these hitters may have exhibited batting averages closer to .400 or even .500. It is from overperformance like this where the ego is built. It is this same ego that carries this individual into a professional career where failure two-thirds of the time is acceptable.

This is also seen in basketball, football, hockey, and soccer; different numbers, but failure outpaces success at the micro level of play throughout. Yet the one thing that keeps these professionals going, besides the million-dollar paychecks, is their ego. Sadly, it is this same ego that gives us arrogant sports figures who feel entitled to use that fame and fortune to spread conflict and turmoil. We hear about cheating, abuse, and excess that is destructive to the players, their families, and their fans who often emulate their behavior.

The final display of ego's negative and positive impact is in politics. I am of the opinion that 20 percent of all politicians are narcissists fed by their ego. It is these 20 percent that ruin the political atmosphere. Think about this: Of the more than 535 members of current and past Congress members from both houses, how many do we actually hear from on a regular basis? When you really think about these vocal and "active" politicians, a high percentage of them are so opinionated that they lack understanding of what is really happening at the grassroots level. They are enamored with their own voice and reflection and don't really connect with most Americans. Yet, the media in its own egotistical actions prop up the most egotistical as those who speak for the citizenry. Quietly, however, behind the scenes, the other 80 percent try to accomplish what they can for their constituents, those who live in the states or districts within the states that the members represent.

Ego is what drives this system. Listen to politicians speak; they will say "I" more than "we" or "us." Look at how they act and vote; it's more about their belief, not the beliefs of the people they represent. Whenever I see state representatives pushing a message nationally, I always question their motivation; I ask, "What does this have to do with where they are from? Who gains from their actions; the politician and his party or the people they represent?" Then I think, "How do I choose what is important to me, what is driving my decisions to be vocal?" This is where I look in the mirror and challenge myself to be true to not only me but to those I influence directly.

Self-Reflection: Looking at Your Internal Mirror

The first time I attempted to reflect on my past, I can honestly say, it scared me[2]. To this day, there is a huge black hole in my childhood. In 2014, I moved my family back to the area in Illinois where I grew up. Today I am surrounded by people I grew up with, some of them since I was five-years-old. Every day of the workweek I drive through West Dundee and see the homes where I grew up. These interactions have helped shine a light in to

---

2 The act of self-reflection can/may recall things that are very unpleasant and may require counsel from a professional psychologist. Self-reflection may uncover the root of personality traits that include abuses or incidents of trauma that trigger subsequent mental health issues. If you are or become aware of any memories that cause you any mental trauma or distress, please seek that help immediately.

that black hole and catch a glimpse of memories that continue to refine who I am today.

My advice for self-recollection is writing or documenting a life timeline. (Creating a life timeline means documenting your life in a time-line-like form with events that occurred over the years. Below you will see an example of mine.) My original recollection activity was centered around my insecurity about change. In 1996, when I started IA, we lived in our first Thornton, Colorado, home. At the time, that home was in a state of disrepair; we were fixing it up, and my life at home and work was in a constant state of change. I was still working for someone else—this was the early days of IA, when we built its foundation.

My primary career at the time was Worldwide IT Manager for a global oil exploration company. The company was traded publicly on the NASDAQ and my work was very visible; I was designing and implementing the computer and ERP systems worldwide. I was thirty-years-old and in a world full of professionals. While I was very good at IT and ERP, I was not good at interacting with professionals from large, nine-figure, publicly traded companies.

The anxiety I felt seemed, at first, to be all mine. However, as I traveled the world implementing our systems in quiet corners like Mount Gilead, Ohio, Jamestown, North Dakota, and Los Reyes, Mexico, I began to experience that same anxiety from the people working at the companies we were acquiring. However, my peers, or people with similar education and age, in places like Houston, Texas, Calgary, Alberta, and New York City had almost no anxiety.

Since my early IA work was focused on developing a standardized procedure to understand, document, and adapt business process and manage change in organizations, I was acutely aware of the anxiety and worked to identify its root cause. From that first day I felt anxiety in myself, I began to self-reflect; this is when I developed my timeline review, or what has now evolved into BizVision.

Self-reflection begins with a timeline: Birth to today. The first timeline review of my life was, itself, revealing. I had never performed this for myself because any time I thought about my childhood all I got was a mind full of nothing. But, sitting at a desk writing out my timeline in 1996, I got this:

> **1966:** Born to young parents - Elgin, Illinois (mom 16, dad 20) (Sherman Hospital)
>
> **Kindergarten:** Immanuel Lutheran - East Dundee, Illinois (Age?) (5) (5–6) (1971–1972) (Move)
>
> **1st Grade:** Immanuel Lutheran - East Dundee, Illinois (Age 6–7) (1972–1973) (Stayed with my teacher at her home, felt secure)
>
> **2nd Grade:** Immanuel Lutheran - East Dundee, Illinois (Age 7–8) (1973–1974)
>
> **3rd Grade:** Immanuel Lutheran - East Dundee, Illinois (Age 8–9) (1974–1975)

By the way, each parenthetical term or phrase represents another recollection that had occurred. This happened in a single sitting, not over a long period of time.

> **4th Grade:** Immanuel Lutheran - East Dundee, Illinois (Age 9–10) (1975–1976) (Kiss first girl) (Call teacher a bitch, get hit in head by her)

Here is where my first "ah-ha" moment occurred!

> **4th Grade:** Move to Wood Dale, Illinois (Parents split up) (We live with aunt) (Zion Lutheran School) (Age 9, 1975) (Hit in head by teacher)

5th Grade: Move to Itasca, Illinois (Age 10–11) (1975–1976) (No baseball) (Live in apartments) (Ridiculed by kids at St. Luke Lutheran)

6th Grade: Move back to Dundee, Illinois (Parents get remarried) (Age 11–12) (1976–1977)

7th Grade: Immanuel Lutheran - East Dundee, Illinois (Parents get divorced) (Mom leaves for California) (Age 12–13) (Move)

7th Grade: Move to California in April (Attend first public school, Los Cerritos, in Thousand Oaks, California) (Age 13) (New stepfather)

8th Grade: Move back to Dundee, Illinois (Stay in public schools: Dundee Middle School) (New stepmother who is 20, my age 13–14)

9th Grade: Dundee High School - Carpentersville, Illinois (New brother) (Strive for friends and am part of "in" group at DHS) (Age 14–15)

10th Grade: Move to Thousand Oaks, California (Attend Thousand Oaks High School) (Age 15–16)

11th Grade: Thousand Oaks High School - Thousand Oaks, California (Age 16–17)

12th Grade: Thousand Oaks High School - Thousand Oaks, California (Age 17–18)

That entire exercise took me about five minutes, but it opened up my mind to things I had not thought about. For example, my "ah-ha" moment was: Wow, I moved a lot.

Mapping yourself does not need to be a complex process. I've seen books and other advisors advocate mapping out your entire self and creating a large list to focus on. As you are aware, I am of the opinion that multi-tasking is a very bad thing. This means that affecting change in yourself needs to be singular in action; get one thing fixed and move on to the next.

To this day, I cannot recall how I felt back in grade school. But I have added to my timeline over the past twenty-two years, especially since moving back to where I spent a lot of my early years. What I initially realized back in 1996 was that my anxiety was fueled by eight moves from kindergarten to twelfth grade and seven schools, including three elementary, two middle, and two high schools. Also, my parents divorced, remarried each other, divorced, remarried other people, and then added to our family; my anxiety about change became clear in that first five-minute recollection.

Identifying the root of an issue is not always easy. What do we do with that knowledge once we have it? I know that, for me, as soon as I identified what was causing my anxiety about change at the core, that anxiety was not as intense the next time it was triggered; but that is not a solution.

I continued to search for a way to incorporate my new knowledge and use it to develop a way to effect and manage change in the workplace. Obvious to me was to finish my timeline, add to it, and expand my past's influence over who I was. What made me such a natural salesperson? What drove me to work hard but procrastinate most important tasks until almost the last moment? Why did I have a propensity to listen to others? How was it that at age thirty, without any real mentor, I could be so pragmatic about business issues? And why did I hate surprises, any kind of surprises?

Self-reflection is also about understanding your everyday actions and reactions. The questions I initially came up with were for those things that were at the top of my mind at the time. As my life has changed, my questions have changed, and the challenge of self-reflection repeats regularly.

As I write this book and look at my team's comments throughout my writing, I am stuck to identify how to apply such a personal and inward-looking task as self-reflection to the various people who will be reading this. I think the first question you should tackle is, *Why am I self-reflecting?*

What is it that is challenging you to discover or rediscover that which is pointing you towards self-reflection? As you determine the root cause of your desire to self-reflect, begin to write down those things, feelings, challenges in a journal or someplace where you can read it back to yourself. The act of finding what is driving you to self-reflect may prove simple or amazingly daunting; whatever it is, continue to let your mind flow along and write down what your mind brings you.

When I did this, I was led to create a timeline. Time is something we all can follow, and a timeline can trigger memories, good and bad. Nonetheless, it's what began my journey. For you, it may not be a timeline but a single event. The events may be sparse and far apart; regardless, once you begin to write them down, you have a puzzle on paper that you can fill in as you go. It may or may not be date sequential; in fact, I have often been focused on an event that happened in my thirties only to be bounced to a memory from my childhood. That is how the human mind works— randomly—and why I recommend writing it all down.

Other questions you can ask yourself:

Why am I friends with . . . ?

Why do I live in . . . ?

Why did I make the decision to . . .?

What influences me to be . . . ?

Why am I influenced by the things that influence me?

For context, I know why I live in Illinois. I know why I choose to remain friends with people whom others may deem unwise. I know why I make decisions; sometimes it's for selfish reasons and other times it's not, but I understand my decision-making process now. I know what influences me, good and bad.

Self-reflection will be the most intimate thing you will ever do. It may scare you. It may anger you. It will change you. Only you can control what you ask yourself. You can choose not to write things down and risk maintaining those gaps in your life in which answers to those questions that may help you or those you influence are missing. Self-reflection in the end is about accepting who you are at the moment you ask those questions, because regardless of who you are now, you will be different tomorrow.

Roots

Earlier I mentioned that a client recently asked me why I do what I do, or why I want to help them. The question came during a discussion about organizational development and realizing their value proposition to their organization. The client asked me why I would spend a full day working with their type of company, then fly to Dallas the next day to work with another small company, then turn around and fly back to them the next day. Essentially, the client wanted to know why I would do all of this when I am the owner of a consulting firm and many other companies.

My answer is simple; I like consulting. However, the three people asking me were executives at a large manufacturing company; they were looking for what motivated me on a deeper level. During my own self-reflection, I learned that I was often alone to make decisions and fend for myself. I had to find a way to overcome the generalizations and stereotypes that went along with my particular situation. Working only for the money is as shallow as dating a good-looking person only because they have good looks. I realized a long time ago that I did not want others to feel that isolation you get when you're left to solve problems you're not quite capable of solving on your own.

It is this motivation that has created my passion for helping people be the best they can be for the companies they work with. There are many ways to help people, but at work people face challenges unique to human development. We all need work to meet the basic needs of our lives: food, shelter, security. If we are unsuccessful in our ability to be effective at work, we risk our very livelihood. I learned that to provide people with the best opportunity to be self-sufficient, helping them have and be the most productive they can be at work will help to ensure that their basic human needs will be fulfilled.

As my motivation carried me from company to company, my understanding of the complexity of human interaction and the challenges businesses face in creating environments for us to work together effectively was transparent. My passion to develop my own skills in helping others understand how to do and be better for themselves and their company is rooted in my childhood.

This passion has led me to a lot of dead ends, and I often felt like I was in a maze, not really knowing where I was going or how to get there. The challenges of developing my own self often interfered with my motivation and replaced my passion with single-mindedness and loathing. I would get the same pushback from the people I was trying to help that I got as a child from the kids who would not accept me. As I child, I had to find a way to manipulate the situation; surely, I could do that as an adult.

In my younger days, I used bragging and pretending to be someone I was not as a way to overcome this. I felt that if I could fit in without actually having the foundation to do so, I could overcome the challenges I was facing.

When René and I were younger, we became friends with a couple who were a little older than us and who had a child a few years older than Mary. This couple had affluent parents, and it showed, from the cars they drove, to the clothes they wore, to the friends they kept. This couple introduced us to their friends; all of them were, as we generalize in America, snobs.

René and I looked up to these people and we did all we could to fit in. However, we did not have the resources to keep up at the pace of this group. This inability to keep up forced us to make decisions; we overspent on things to help us appear to be more like them. When we were together, I would talk about the wins I had, even exaggerating those wins to elevate my stories to a level these people could accept and respect; they saw right through it and never quite accepted us.

Through my life, it is this cycle of trying to fit in that has taught me the lessons and helped me to create the habits I needed to accept who I am and what my value proposition is to myself: my family, friends, companies, and clients. Value is not a dollar amount; it's that reward we get by achieving our goals, the thing that motivates us to keep doing what we like and find a way to shed that which we don't.

Self-realization is about linking your motivation to your experiences and finding the passion within that to propel you forward one moment at a time. Self-realization is your chance at resetting the events that you feel have been holding you back and turning them into the fuel that drives you to the next phase of learning and growth. Self-realization is using those memories to stay the course and not digress or abandon that which you know is right and good. Self-realization is identifying your mistakes and not repeating them or working out solutions to those mistakes and making them right if need be.

As you continue to take this journey back through your life experiences, there may more than one self-realization that happens; who you want to be as a person.

Who Do You Want to Be?

I think it's humorous when people ask children who they want to be when they grow up. The innocence of the answers from children remind us that life should be so simple as to choose our future purely on the basis of the passion we feel. Children answer these questions knowing only that being a policeman, fireman, or what their parents do makes them feel, generally, very good. Why is it that when we get older, we change our view of who we want to be?

When I was a kid, my father was a fireman. He was the first paramedic in West Dundee in the 1970s. I grew up in the early days being around firemen and fire trucks. As you have read, however, my childhood was not overly memorable for reasons I still struggle to comprehend. As my own self-reflection has progressed, I have become more understanding of who I want to be, and it has very little to do with a career or job.

Growing up, we were poor. I ate peanut butter sandwiches every day. I also attended a private Lutheran school and was surrounded by kids from affluent or upper-middle-class families. I wanted to have what they had, which at the time seemed to me to be money. That was the easiest answer for an elementary school-aged child: I wanted a nice house, hot meals, nice clothes, and nice cars.

Sometime in my early elementary school years, I determined that I wanted to be an accountant. Through elementary school, middle school, and high school I continued to be surrounded by affluent people, and their influence continued to push me to make decisions based solely on the material things that money provided. For me, the answer to, Who do you want to be? was, A person who mattered to those within my areas of influence. In my early years, the only way for me to get what I felt I needed was either to have money or to be perceived as having money. This turned me into someone I did not want to be.

My striving to fit in with a certain clique, and then getting into that clique, did not fulfill my quest for who I wanted to be; I just kept making bad decisions. In high school, I decided I needed more money to get better influence over the people I wanted acceptance from. To do that, I got into drugs. My dive into drugs gave me what I thought I wanted and made me who I thought I wanted to be: a leader.

As I expanded my area of influence, I abandoned those things that I had previously had passion for: baseball, relationships, family. In return for this, I got money and things and false friends who liked my things but not the person I was. These choices led to my joining the military—a 180-degree turn from who I wanted to be, but a necessity for my emotional and physical development at this phase in my life.

During my time in the military, I still could not have told you who I wanted to be, except to say that I wanted to be accepted. I graduated top of my class in AIT; then, just as I was about to receive the rewards of my accomplishments in the army, my life changed again. This was a direct result of actions that I do not regret but wish I had understood better at the time. Regardless, my focus on being an accountant was revitalized during my time in the military.

Who I wanted to be was further complicated during this time, as I met my first wife, Vanessa, while I was in the military. This chance meeting resulted in my amazing daughter, Kristin, who has been an inspiration and catalyst for much of who I am today. However, the introduction of a relationship in the middle of the turmoil of being in the military, learning how to be an adult, and wanting to be an accountant, created challenges in my quest for who I felt I wanted to be.

My marriage with Vanessa failed; it was doomed before it began. Nevertheless, my career as an accountant would be launched in part because of this relationship; it was my need to support my family that brought me to the man who would help define much of who I am professionally: Jack Danger.

Jack helped me to understand, better than anyone, who I wanted to be. He hired me to install a computerized accounting system at a time when computerized accounting systems were not the norm. The integration of accounting, computers, the task-driven programming, and teaching people to use the systems brought who I wanted to be into focus for the first time: a person who integrated people, process, and technology. More than that, Jack showed me that success did not come from stuff; it came from character, perseverance, and empathy.

This was in 1988, and while I had learned who I wanted to be, I had not learned how to become who I wanted to be. It would take me another eight years to grasp the true concept of applying the lessons of my life to the intentions I would create for myself. During those eight years, I learned about who I was and how where I came from contributed to that. I learned about how my decisions affected myself, my family, and those I influence. I have since learned how to continue using the tools of self-reflection, honesty, and intention to remain true to who I want to be and what I will become.

I want to help people realize their potential in team environments and be recognized for doing that. Becoming who I want to be evolved from chasing physical wealth, to being accepted, to learning about accounting and computers, to helping individuals understand how to work with computers and other individuals around them to make the entire company better. This entire process led me to Individual Advantages and fulfillment of who I always wanted to be: accepted as a leader who is part of something bigger than myself but recognized for my contribution within it.

Who you want to be is not about some physical job or position; it is not about the physical things you may acquire doing that job. Who you want to be is about how you proceed with your life on a daily basis and about how those actions make you feel; it's about what you end up doing in relation to the influences you have and receive.

As you read this book and begin to formulate questions that are individual to you, the answers to those questions will show you who you want to be. With these answers, you can look more clearly at who you have become and who you are. My hope is that it will be easy for you to construct questions for yourself because you know yourself best.

Who you want to be is affected by how you want to be perceived and what influences you will have, as well as what influences you. Who you become will be defined by these things, too. Your actions as an individual, and within your Individual environments, also define who you are. You can change who you want to be and/or reach your goals to become who you want to be by applying the lessons of this book. The journey you take will be created by your own review and application of these rules, each influencing the end result.

Self-Deception

We all do it and we do it often. Sometimes the lies we tell ourselves are white lies. Spending money, spending time, delay of action, or speed of action. We've all spent money we should not have spent and convinced ourselves that we can afford it. We've committed to do something in a certain amount of time and told ourselves, "I can get this done by this time." We've all said, "I don't have to start that task right now, I can finish in time." Or, "I can quickly get through this task," but you cannot. The examples are infinite; we lie to ourselves regularly.

Why do we lie to ourselves? The primary reason is ego. It makes us feel better to hide behind the lies and convince ourselves that picking up the pieces left after we continue to do self-destructive things is easier than correcting the self-destructive behavior. *Change* may be the single most difficult word for humans, especially if change challenges the status quo, even a status quo that is destructive.

We can often justify our actions or words by playing games with specifics, or use of language, or my favorite: Point of View. The fact is that we humans have a gift to use context in our communication and by doing so can alter perception to sway things our way. Lying to yourself doesn't give you anything positive in return. It may provide you with the immediate gratification of being right or happy, but when you look at the bigger picture, you will find that any form of lying to yourself is only holding you back from being the best *you* you can be.

The act of lying to ourselves to feel better is a human frailty that has no boundary. Dishonesty to ourselves and others damages our credibility and makes us inconsistent; inconsistency is itself a form of dishonesty. Our ability to trick ourselves and accept mediocrity is what hinders our ability to take advantage of all the individual advantages that present themselves in our life.

I still fail to adhere to my own convictions; to fail is to be human. Being honest requires hard work and patience with yourself. I guarantee you will lie to yourself for the rest of your life, but the healthy thing to do is to hold yourself accountable for your internal actions.

If you want to be honest with yourself, you must first ask why you lie in the first place. What is motivating you to be dishonest with yourself and then with others? What is it that needs to be achieved? My motivation was wanting to be accepted. Since I found out early that perception is reality, it's easy to create a false perception. What would happen if you cleared the smoke and smashed the mirrors and just were you?

For some, being *you* may be being gregarious, high-profile, and bois-terous. René is the most friendly and outgoing person I have ever known. When René walks into a room, she can steal the show; her enthusiasm and pure happiness is almost overpowering—at times, I feel like a bump on a log. René is also naturally beautiful; she is blessed with that rare combina-tion of inner and outer beauty that everyone sees and feels.

However, there are some people who see René and think, "This can-not be her true self; this must be an act." Those of us who know her know that this is the real René; there is no wavering in her personality nor in how she presents herself to the world. The Ney Sayers learn this pretty fast. (Pun intended: I call René "Ney.")

I've often wondered how René came to be this beautiful person. Where does this inner beauty come from? Recently, René shared with me that she is terrified by new situations; they make her uncomfortable and create a high level of anxiety; I was floored. I took some time to think about this and wondered, Could it be that René has been faking who she is all this time?

Reflecting on almost twenty-eight years together, I knew the answer was no; René is as honest about herself as she is with others. Her amazing personality is driven by her anxiety, but that anxiety just turbo charges her friendliness and ability to warm a relationship. René is who she is and does not put on airs or have a pretentious bone in her body. She shields her anxiety, yes, but in doing so she has not created a false persona or developed traits that negatively affect others. It enhances her foundational personality without altering it.

As for me, that kind of anxiety management and self-confidence took half a lifetime to acquire. I would often justify my behavior in my own mind, lying to myself along the way. I bought cars I should not have bought, wore clothes that gave off a certain look, and participated in functions that I despised but embraced as if they were who I was, all to provide the world with a perception that I was better. What I did not realize is that people liked me for who I was without those actions, and I would have more true friends today had I understood this act of self-deception much sooner.

In the end, you will need to figure out what is real and what is not. As you begin to slow down and self-reflect, your focus will become clearer and you will be able to distinguish between the things that provide you with a false image and a true image. Whatever choice you make, if you're honest about the choice, is probably going to support who you ultimately want to be.

Intuition

Throughout your life, you will have opportunities. The more you know yourself and incorporate slowing down, the more advantages you will create that provide opportunities. You may be saying, "How does self-reflection and slowing down work? How do I know if an opportunity is the right opportunity? Are there ways to know if they are not the right one?" I think there are, and the first thing you need to do is listen internally to your emotions.

Challenge opportunities that are a result of pure emotion. Emotions can interfere with our ability to create advantages in our decisions or actions. Reactive tendencies often eliminate opportunity by alienating us from people or opportunity that might otherwise provide additional advantages to us. What is fueling the emotion, and how urgent is the emotion that is driving you to make a decision?

Self-reflection is a good tool when this occurs because you may discover a secret agenda buried in your mind that conflicts with your current life, or worse, is something that you should not be doing. This may be the most difficult to differentiate, but let's look at my own history of emotional decisions that have altered or delayed my purpose in life so far.

Baseball will be the crux of my lesson here. I have previously mentioned my love for baseball. I so loved the game that at twenty-eight I embarked on a quest to play Major League Baseball—despite my age and the fact that I had not been playing at any professional competitive level. At the time, I had been married for under two years and my business was young but stable. René was pregnant with Mary, and I was not in the best shape of my life. So, why did I do this? Ego.

I was a good baseball player as a kid. I had a friend who was drafted into MLB right out of high school. My business provided me an opportunity to work with baseball players and teams, giving me the idea that maybe I could play. So, as you've read, I tried. During my time in Florida playing in Spring Training Tryouts for the Houston Astros, I was injured. I had to go to the hospital and ended up in a sling, out of the tryouts. But I had good memories and some very cool experiences, and I wasn't ready to give up on baseball.

As soon as we got back to Colorado, I began looking to play ball on a competitive team. I landed in a local semi-pro league and, with my training to try out at MLB camps, was good enough to make the All-Star team in the league. At this time, MLB was going through some issues—a strike was looming—and I felt like I had a shot at playing as a scab player. (*Scab* is the common, usually unflattering, term for a person who crosses the picket line of protesting union workers.) However, life had different plans for me. I was in a car accident, hit by a drunk driver, and both of my wrists were so severely injured that I needed three operations.

Now, you'd think I would be done, but I love baseball. A couple years later, I had another opportunity. I had a friend who played on a competitive baseball team. At the time I was thirty-four, and our companies were doing pretty well. Henry was a baby and Mary was six, and my infatuation with golf after moving onto a golf course was waning. I joined the team and immediately had a position; my ability to play well came back quickly and I was identified as one of the top players and was again nominated to play on the All-Star team. Once again, just as I felt I was hitting my stride, something happened; my thumb was crushed to the point where my thumb bone was broken in over eight pieces.

Did this incident give me pause? Do you think I slowed down enough or reflected on my history in baseball? Nope. When we moved to Oregon, there was another team. This team was ranked second in the United States in its league, and I would be the oldest player by over fourteen years, but I started. This time I made it through about two-thirds of the season before my left rotator cuff and bicep muscle tore; then, I was done.

It was at this time that I did one of my self-reflections and saw clearly that sports, specifically baseball, were not meant to be in my life. Looking back over my timeline I could trace this issue back to 1978, when I moved from Illinois to California for the first time. One of the main reasons I decided to move was to get away from the issues I was having with baseball in Illinois. Those issues continued to show themselves through high school and then into my adult life, over and over, but my ego and going too fast got in the way for over twenty years.

The conclusion of my attempt to stay connected to baseball happened in 2016. I was afforded the opportunity to coach at my original high school, where I played in ninth grade. As a sophomore, Henry was playing on the team and I was asked to help—a dream for me. Within eight weeks of agreeing, I threw out my right rotator cuff and ended up with more surgery. Even after learning my lesson to not play, I hadn't connected the dots to understand I was not supposed to be involved in baseball at all—ever.

Life gives us signs when we slow down and pay attention. Now, I'm not saying that every bad thing that happens is a sign to not do something. But if you are trying to do something, and repeatedly you are given a sign that it's not the right thing for you, pay attention. This is where slowing down and being honest with yourself can come into play. I know today that I get just as much enjoyment watching as I do participating in baseball. My need to participate was fueled by my need to be in control and stemmed from what I perceived as a position of influence. However, I now know that I could have provided positive moments in my own life and others had I yielded sooner to the signs life was giving me.

When challenges are presented, pause to ask yourself why you are being challenged. What is the challenge? Under what context is it being provided? It's okay, and normal, to struggle with reaching your goals; things that come easily should be reflected on just as much as things that come with difficulty. The more thought and planning you put into your life's decisions, the more fluid those decisions will appear. However, we can get into a comfortable focus in those things that we feel we know well, allowing part of our ego to take over, potentially creating struggles and obstacles in our path due to our own arrogance, insecurity, difficulty following through, ignorance, or stupidity.

Regardless of how good or bad your path is, you must understand that path and how you got there before you can really move forward honestly and with the real influence you need to evolve in a positive way; understanding where you are in the present is the clarity we all need as humans to progress.

Clarity

Recollection is about clarity. Clarity about who you are and eventually about your purpose here in this life. We all have a purpose to be here, and by gaining clarity about your past you have a better chance at understanding and accepting that purpose. Now, this is not about settling. I believe that each and every person has a specific purpose. That includes being the best we can be as individuals and giving something that enhances the Individuals we influence, and we all have influence.

I've written about my initial recollection and how some follow-up recollections have clarified some issues in my life. But baseball is not where I will leave this lesson. My life path has led me to this point where I have the foundation, experience, and knowledge to share with the world why Individual Advantages are neither singular nor plural; it has been and will always be cyclical and all-encompassing, and it will reach every single human on Earth today and in the future.

In the early days of IA, I felt like I needed a foundation for my concepts. At first, I had no idea where to begin. Up until 1996, I had been primarily an IT/accounting guy installing computerized accounting systems and not really paying specific attention to my past or its effect on anything.

My lessons about business process and the complexities of human interaction in the workplace were even lost on the speed of doing business in the mid-1990s. My focus was on making money, speeding up the workplace, and making it more efficient.

Life was showing me signs at the same time. Up to 1995, I had not traveled much. Beginning in 1996, I was flying all over the world, and by 1999 those travels had increased to over 100,000 miles a year. At that same time we built a home, Mary entered kindergarten, and IA had taken shape. I was also fully committed to my doctoral studies and doing a lot of research on human interaction between workers and technology. Through this research, I kept reflecting on the parallels in my life and each time dove as deep as my memory would allow.

One of the issues that I struggled with was my connection to my parents. If we are shaped by our past, what kind of parent and then what kind of leader would I be? As you have read, my childhood was chaotic and, in further recollection, unstructured until eighth grade. I recalled in mid- to late 1999 the structure that was introduced to me by my stepparents, Bill and Michele. Each came into my life at about the same time and brought a certain amount of structure that neither my sister nor I had had up to that point. In fact, I cannot recall any structure whatsoever, to the point that one of my memories is downright frightening.

I must have been in third or fourth grade, and it was fall. At the time, we lived right next door to Highlands Elementary School (the public elementary school in West Dundee), but we (my sister and I) attended Immanuel (the private Lutheran school). We were not generally accepted by the kids in the neighborhood; in fact, I was bullied a lot. One day my sister and I were sitting in the house alone (mind you, she is three years younger than me). As the kids from Highlands walked by, I spied them through the scope of my father's 30.06 deer rifle, while it was attached to the rifle. I don't recall where my parents were, but I do recall the feelings of that time; emptiness and loneliness, as I think we were left to our own devices even at that age.

You may ask why this story resonates in my mind about lack of structure. My parents were very young and, I suspect, did not realize what my sister and I were enduring. What resonated with me was the ridicule and bullying of both of us from the kids who walked by my home every day. I could not defend my sister against all who would bully her, and I lacked the confidence to stand up to those who bullied me. Struggling to make ends meet, raise a young family, and provide a private education, my young parents had no clue what my sister or I were going through, and they could not really protect us. While I do not blame my parents individually, I do realize that they did not understand at the time that the lack of parental structure provided me with the psyche to pick up a rifle and view those kids who tormented us and imagine I could ward them off from the safety of my living room.

As I recollect this story, I am struck by the news of recent school shootings; could I have been one of those shooters? What signs are being missed by parents, teachers, and other people of influence that might help to resolve the demons created by the actions of human against human? What demons did this event and those that led to me pointing a rifle at children, as a child, survive into my adult life? I know that to this day I am protective of my sister and anyone else who is bullied or picked on. I always root for the underdog. I can adapt, and have adapted, to almost any situation; I have a tremendous sense of situational awareness when presented with a new environment or changes to my current environment. I accept people, good and bad, for who they are at the time and believe that each person can be better. Most of all, my ability to empathize has been the single biggest benefit of this event. My ability to empathize and help others do the same may be one of the biggest influencers in life.

Our journey together is just beginning. So far we have explored who we are and how who we are forms the building blocks of our foundation. We should have a glimpse of what we face within ourselves at this point; that glimpse is part of our foundation. Keep these realizations at the top of your mind as we continue to dive deeper into your individual.

4.0

Foundation

*"When the roots are deep, there is no reason
to fear the wind." - African proverb*

BEING SELF-AWARE IS A CORNERSTONE OF YOUR FOUNDA-tion. Knowing who you are today and how your past has influenced you should never be neglected again. I have heard many people say, "I want to forget the past." I personally don't think that's healthy. Recalling the past ensures that you have a chance to not repeat mistakes. The past offers us opportunity. Being self-aware of how your past is manifested in your present will help you to refine your actions.

We are a product of our environment, which for humans includes our family, friends, community, culture, socioeconomic status, education, religion, political influences, career, and overall day-to-day life experiences. Being able to grow to be and exercise a positive influence despite a past that is dark and traumatic is the ultimate form of living positively. Resilience to the darkest parts of the world is how we can all become more present and more aware. All of these products contribute to our personality, mannerisms, character traits, and thought process, and being aware of each of these is the foundation of being self-aware.

When you can set aside your ego and be honest with yourself about who you are, inside and out, you will be able to see your true foundation. Our foundations may have cracks; we may have habits and character flaws that we want to dispose of or change, but how can you begin to shore up your foundation if you don't first learn what it's made of? To change, to be better for yourself and those you influence, you must look into your internal mirror and find your foundation.

Self-Awareness

Why, you ask, would we want to dive so deep into our past to discuss our psychological foundation in a book about Individualism? Your foundation can have weak points that will need to be shored up. Your foundation as a leader will need to support you, your family, and all of those people you influence. The load you put on your personal foundation will change often through your life, and if you're not prepared to recognize the flaws when they appear and shore them up, you and those you influence can be negatively affected.

Understanding how our past has affected who we are today, in this moment, is critical to moving forward. For those of us who are happy with where we are, refining or polishing our present self can be aided by self-awareness. For those of us who have issues we wish to resolve, self-awareness can help us get past the mental barriers holding us back. Many of us have emotional baggage holding us back, memories that stir emotions that affect our way of communicating with ourselves and others. When emotions dictate how we communicate, how we communicate becomes ineffective and is often destructive to our foundation.

I hate surprises, all surprises. Any action that can be deemed a surprise has the potential to instill in me rapid negative emotion. Why? How is it that I can I be calm, focused, and intentional and with a single surprise have my entire day derailed?

There are a few defining moments in my childhood that led me to the source of my dislike of surprises. First is my fourth-grade move from West Dundee (Immanuel Lutheran) to Wood Dale (Zion Lutheran). Moving is hard for any child; learning about the move one day before it happens is traumatic. I was already an angry child; I was surrounded by people who seemed to have stability—like my classmates—and my life significantly lacked that, except for attending school, a constant that was suddenly upended. My life timeline shows clear signs of my uneasiness about change that stems from moving; a common factor is that each of my subsequent moves was also a surprise to me. Each surprise move contributed to my next phase of needing control; I needed to fix my instability.

When I unexpectedly moved to California at the end of seventh grade, I forced myself to make a decision in light of my instability; I moved back to Illinois before the eighth grade. My eighth-grade and ninth-grade school years were stable but marked by the surprise of my father's marrying a woman who was only seven years older than me. That event never evolved into a good experience for me, and in order to prevent further surprises, I moved back to California right before tenth grade.

My chaotic decision making was my attempt to remain in control; these decisions were primarily made out of rash determination instead of patience or perseverance of situations that were uncomfortable for me at the time. I would alter my future to remain in control, good or bad.

Sometime after meeting René this changed for me. René became an anchor that allowed me to search for more decisions, like her, that would continue to ground me mentally and physically. Even though I recognize this today, this was not a conscious decision on my part; I did not realize this fact until the early 2000s.

One of the most memorable and unpleasant surprises for me was my thirtieth birthday party. It was 1996, and professionally I was in transition. IA would not become a legal entity for a couple more weeks. The idea behind IA was new, and I was mentally preoccupied. I had just sold our accounting system implementation business, was working for the company that bought it, and began to travel more frequently. One day, I came home to a house full of people; a surprise party.

The first person I saw was a classmate from Thousand Oaks High School who had never been a close friend, and to see him intensified the discomfort of surprise. Our home was a work in process, I was a work in process, our marriage was a work in process with a new child; it was one of the worst events of my adult life.

You'd think such an event with family and friends would be good, but no. To this day, I still don't like surprises of any kind, good or bad. This awareness has become more important as my responsibility to others has increased. My reaction to surprises is now less tumultuous. I channel the emotion into the proper place to not create surprise moments for others by my actions; believe me, some people don't take too kindly when your reaction to surprise events is counter to what is expected.

When you have reactions that are so immediate, such as negative emotions, and you want to control them or stop them from happening, you are going to need to make that a habit.

Habits

We all have habits, good and bad. Habits are those automatic repetitive actions that will ultimately define you, to yourself and to others. Habits will contribute greatly to your ability to succeed, fail, fit in, and be happy or sad. Habits are part of the advantages or disadvantages of life. Simple habits that seem personal to us, in that they don't have a direct influence on others, can actually prove to have a dramatic effect. Certain habits with a physical aspect everyone can relate to in one way or another: biting nails, skin picking, hair pulling, etc. These are well-studied habits and are classified as Body-Focused Repetitive Behaviors (BFRB).

René and I both bite our nails, and I also skin pick at my fingers; too much information, right? This is a habit that really has no impact on a third party. The fact that my nails are short and some skin is picked away has no bearing on my ability to be a good consultant. However, the unsightly appearance can be off-putting to people who judge others critically for such a habit; thus, it could have a direct effect that is unintended or even undeserved.

Only one of our children is a nail biter, so does this habit have a genetic component or is it, through observation, a learned trait? How do you overcome these habits in support of creating more advantages for yourself? Another habit is the use of common phrases or words. When I met René, she used the word "whatnot" all the time when speaking; however, she did not use the word when writing. Why is this?

Understanding habits can help us to solve those things in our life we wish to change. If we can identify a habit we dislike and work to change that habit, we will make progress and we will create new advantages for ourselves. If we observe a behavior we'd like to develop in ourselves, we can arrange to spend the time and effort to repeat the task to the point that it becomes habit. Habit can even be used to overcome certain addictions, which are really just dependent habits in the end.

Do something consistently for three to six weeks and it will become a habit. There are exceptions to this, but generally speaking it holds true. If you ever want to change something in your life, all that you need to do is repeat the desired action for three to six weeks and you will have made the change habitual. The hard part will be holding yourself accountable to sticking to what is needed to keep going as your life changes and adapts to the new action.

This applies to almost anything. Want to start working out at a certain time on certain days? Find a way to work out on those days for three to six weeks without any interruption, and your chances of doing it consistently in the future will be very high. I used this to create the habit of reading trade rags. I needed a way to stay well read on the various industries that I consult to. The amount and variety of information I needed to know was growing so fast that unless I found a way to keep up I was at risk of becoming irrelevant. Over time, it has become a habit for me to read trade rags so that our company can remain relevant; I never miss an issue.

Look around and you will notice patterns. Patterns are consistencies. You and others have patterns that are individual to yourself. Your family, friends, and peers all have certain patterns that affect you, and you have patterns that affect them. Patterns can be synonymous to habits, and it's important to understand the patterns. If you are mimicking actions of others—that is following a pattern—that will eventually become a habit.

Businesses we work with often don't have policies and procedures, they have habits. These habits are the way they do things to keep the company going, but they are not written down or documented—it's just the way they do it. When new people come into the organization and mimic what others are doing, their actions become new habits. These patterns may or may not be efficient or healthy for the business or people, yet they do them over and over, repeating even the most difficult and frustrating tasks because "it's the way it's always been done."

This is the trap that habits can spring on us. We get so comfortable with what we are doing that we are numb to its effects. These effects can extend to our character and personality. By identifying habits or patterns, you can correctly put them into perspective and use them to effect change and create more advantages.

Character

Character is the measurement of your personality or way you are. Character matters in almost all you do. Personality is a tad frivolous; it's an appearance or our image. A person's character can be impugned or enhanced but not determined by one's personality. Personality is your outward visible self and can be altered at a whim, character is earned. Personality and character are both influenced by your inner self; however, your outer self is what controls the perception of the public. You can spend your whole life building your character and in one action change the perception of it. How people label your character may not be what your character truly is; your personality can mask or improve your character and even fool people into believing your character is something it is not.

You can define or identify someone's personality as, for example, serious, shy, lazy, outgoing. These personality traits can lead to a character assessment; for example, a serious person may be deemed to have good character because the person appears to be sincere and approach things thoughtfully. However, another likewise serious person may be deemed to have a questionable character because the person appears to be overly direct or intrusive. Similarly, a shy person may be deemed to have an arrogant or snobbish character.

The biggest differentiation is time. One can influence emotion quickly with personality, but character can take time. For example, knowing if someone is honest, a character trait, doesn't automatically denote understanding of how that person reacts to issues that measure such a character trait. Being kind or virtuous both require time to measure, while personality traits are something that can be measured almost immediately.

I am often told that I am too direct. I work very hard to be honest in all I do; not being honest has proven to me from experience to be one of the worst things you can be to anyone, including yourself. However, honesty will someday put you in a position to answer a question or tell someone something that will be taken negatively. Honesty is a character trait that almost all people would love to be known for; even liars strive to be thought of as honest.

Being honest can sometimes put the honest person in an awkward position. I have some dramatic examples of being honest that, on the surface, appear mean-spirited. Some issues are everyday and even common-sense, but people looking in from the outside still perceive the honesty as cruel.

We had an IT consultant who worked for us who had horrible halitosis, so bad that being around him was like being around a sewer. I did not work with this person; in fact, I did not hire him and cannot recall being within thirty feet of him in the first three months he worked for us. We began to notice that other consultants shied away from working with him, so I asked our team questions; none shared anything with us. One day, one of my clients called and said he had a complaint about one of our consultants. That complaint was lodged by his staff, who said our consultant had a hygiene issue.

I immediately called his project manager, told the project manager that we had received a complaint about this person and his hygiene, and asked the project manager to please discuss it with him. The reply I received was not acceptable to me because it forced me to handle a situation that is commonsense and, quite frankly, should not be something that goes on for three months.

I sat the consultant down and almost immediately detected the issue; very poor oral hygiene. The thing is that he had white teeth; the issue was apparently much larger than just bad breath. When confronted, the consultant admitted that he had been made aware of the issue for some time. He said he went through bottles of mouthwash and brushed his teeth many times a day. Amazingly, none of the people he worked with at our company said a word to him.

The issue was compounded by the fact this consultant was very good at what he did. His input was requested by his teammates and our clients. The other issue is that he knew he was in demand and thought his superficial approach was enough; as smart as he was, he refused to address the root cause and tried to cover it up with mouthwash and brushing only.

Hearing that he had gone to superficial lengths but not really addressed the root cause of the issue, I relieved him of his work duties until he sought out professional help. He was in disbelief that I would put him on unpaid leave, but his issue was that severe. I told him that he was being penalized not for a physical issue but for a mental issue by not addressing the fact that his halitosis was causing others tremendous discomfort and also affecting the company's reputation. His inability to identify that he had a bigger issue concerned me on more than a few levels. What other issues might this person have bad judgment on?

Acceptance of things that are not generally accepted is a character issue; it's a form of ego and arrogance. For this consultant to think that his mind was so great that people should accept his horrible bad breath is a character flaw. We see this time and again in humans; people expect others to accept bad behavior because they think they are special in some way. There are other ways to damage your character other than connecting the physical self to the mental self.

Working in the field that I do, I have had to be honest with many people about many uncomfortable things. Most of the things I have had to be honest about, I am sure many people would shy away from. As in my previous example, nobody that I worked with would come forward and be honest about this consultant's hygiene issue; even when I asked questions, nobody said anything. Honesty isn't always about bringing people happy news. It's about having enough respect for the other human being to lay it all on the line for them. Sometimes this kind of honesty can label you as an asshole. For me, being labeled as dishonest is a far worse punishment.

Being labeled dishonest will stick with a person; even if the person rebuilds a reputation for being honest, the stigma of being dishonest can rear its ugly head. Personality and character are distinguishable from one another to an extent. A person can change their personality quickly, going from outgoing to introverted or from flirtatious to standoffish depending on the situation.

Another issue with character is that it can be called into question just by the company you keep or the profession you're in. For example, being a politician carries inherent questions from people who oppose or do not share your political affiliation; Democrats often question Republicans' political beliefs and vice versa. Similarly, being an attorney or used car salesperson often comes with challenges to your character as part of long-standing generalizations.

Personality can be changed in moment; you may appear or be labeled happy or sad with a simple change in how an interaction happens. However, changing one's impression of a person's character takes time. Meeting someone and establishing a relationship that identifies character requires time, sometimes months or even years.

Perception Is Reality

Having a questionable character can cause a lot of difficulties for a person. Being labeled as untrustworthy, dishonest, selfish, narcissistic, or spiteful can stay with you for a long time. Identifying a character flaw and alleviating that flaw are both difficult. We have discussed that self-assessment can be difficult; being honest about character issues can prove to be the most difficult. Often we justify our actions that damage our character, forgetting that perception of action and result goes beyond our own definition.

We moved to Klamath Falls, Oregon, in 2005. The move there was easy for me and difficult for my family. René was born and raised in Colorado, and her entire social world was there. Henry was four, so he had not established himself in school or with a large number of friends. Mary, however, was entering sixth grade and had established friendships at a critical time of a young girl's life.

My goal was more time with my family. As a consultant, I traveled a lot and had missed most of my children's life due to work and travel; moving to Oregon was an opportunity to change that. My primary goal in 2005 was working with a client who had contracted me to move to Oregon and personally oversee their business operations; IA kept running in the background and required very little of my time.

As an international consultant moving from Denver to Klamath Falls, I brought with me a perspective of business and leadership that I can say was dramatically different from what a small, rural, mountain community was used to. Employee, vendor, and customer relationships were not similar to those you might see in urban or suburban areas.

Early on, some of my character traits became a challenge to some. First was my direct and up-front way of discussing issues. I would and continue to engage people in direct communication about any issue facing us. I speak honestly about the issue and I do so without emotion. That style of management quickly labeled me an asshole.

Vendors did not like that I would challenge them. There was this one vendor, a food vendor who had done business with the company for five years, who probably had 75 percent of the wholesale food business in town with restaurants. He was well known, a local who had grown up in the area and had a lot of influence.

One of the first things I did upon taking over day-to-day operations was reconcile our purchasing programs and validate our vendor performance and pricing. Food cost was a major concern to me as it was a double-digit percentage higher than it should've been. Inventory and portion controls did not seem to move the needle more than a couple of percentage points over the first few inventory reviews and financial cycles, so I revisited our vendor pricing.

I was visited early in the process by this vendor and challenged as to why I would question his pricing. I explained to him that our cost numbers were higher than they should be and that it was not due to portion or inventory control issues, which left us with original cost of food. The relationship with this vendor ended.

It was not more than five months later that character would enter the picture. In that time, a number of local restaurant owners learned that I was not an employee of the company I was working for but a management consultant. This information became known because during that time it was learned by most owners that I actually had equity in the company, changing my social status from an "outsider manager" to a "local business owner," which opened doors of communication.

One of the first things I offered to these business owners was what we commonly call "low hanging fruit." I told them they should price shop their food vendor. It took one month for my character to be challenged by the status quo in Klamath Falls. I was approached by more than a few who accused me of all sorts of bad things; I was accused of price fixing, unethical business practices, home wrecking (how this one spiraled out I will never know), and being anti-local business, and these turned into liar, cheater, and all-around bad guy. To reiterate my point, all I did was change food vendors to save my company money.

Did you ever play the Telephone Game as a kid? Tell one person a story and when that person tells the next the following iteration of the story will be slightly different. Two things immediately happened as a result of this series of character assassinations: Our food service declined, and I decided that all our local vendors needed to be challenged.

My reputation continued to be attacked. In fact, up to this day you can still find a large number of businesspeople who will tell you that I'm an asshole. Ask them to give you a specific reason, and not one can objectively do so. But perception is reality. I even began to think of myself as an asshole and wore the term like a badge of honor in Klamath Falls. However, this was to be yet another lesson for me, and it took getting to the root of the issues to learn how it would affect my life.

Suffice it to say the business began making money in food operations and all other operations as well. We went on to build a hotel, and during that process I reinforced with a number of local business people the idea that I was—in their mind—an asshole, and they perpetuated that within their spheres of influence. The act of embracing my new label severely damaged my reputation. It affected my partners, my family, and my friends. Perception is reality, and as I reinforced this label through agreement that I was an asshole, my character was perceived as such by all who did not know me well.

What is missing from perception is context. Ever heard that there are three sides to every story? People who heard from the food vendor only heard his side of the story and did not understand the context. I did not help when people would approach me and say, "I heard you're a pretty tough business person, kind of an ass." To which I would say, "Yep, that's me."

My reality is that I want everyone to succeed. I had nothing personal against that food salesman at all, but his prices were too high for my business. In fact, this label followed me on numerous occasions in Klamath Falls for challenging people's price or lack of customer service. I was labeled a lot of things on initial perceptions; all of the labels challenged my character.

I am guilty of all those things that damage character. In my life I have lied, cheated, and stolen. Those decisions do not reflect my character today, and anyone who labels me that way is lost. I am often empathetic with myself, and I think that once you can be empathetic with yourself, your character will improve.

Empathy

When I make a character mistake or see someone I influence make one, I will challenge myself or that person to rectify the issue.

I am involved in an association, IKECA (International Kitchen Exhaust Cleaning Association). One of our companies (Omni Containment Systems) is a manufacturing company and sells to the primary members of this organization. Our company has a tremendous amount of influence in the market, and I have been representing this company at IKECA since 2009.

About five years ago, I began teaching business and leadership sessions at IKECA in the name of Individual Advantages. I wanted to bring to IKECA some of the lessons we teach our clients around the world. My personal influence at IKECA has grown, and my character is as good as anyone's with the same record of membership in the organization.

Omni has a competitor that is also very involved at IKECA. This competitor is a good company that is owned by a larger company and provides very similar products to the kitchen exhaust cleaning (KEC) market. About four years ago, Omni decided to develop a product that could be used in the competitor's system. That system is not patented, so our development was within the normal scope of business. Omni had just finished defending a patent violation on one of our products, and that issue was public, so the company position and my position on intellectual property of any kind was visible and understood by all.

My session to the IKECA membership that day was about leadership. About five minutes before my presentation, the president of the competitor approached me with a piece of paper in his hand. On that paper was a marketing message that introduced our new product to the marketplace, and it also used the competitor's logo. The message had been released to our full distribution network the previous day in support of our marketing efforts at the IKECA show.

The problem was that our message was a potential violation of the competitor's trademark and did not properly identify our product. I was mortified. Here I was standing behind the curtain about to address a couple hundred people about leadership and character and standing in front of me is positive proof that I'm about to become a hypocrite. I did not know what I was going to do. This executive and his team were not happy, clearly, and they had every right to be. I told him and his team that I would make it right, but I did not say how, and I could read the skepticism on their faces.

I began my talk by figuratively falling on my sword. I announced to the entire IKECA membership that Omni violated several promises we had made to them and our entire customer base. I told them it was my responsibility to ensure that we operated according to our promises and that we had failed, and that in doing so we had printed things about our competitor's products that were untrue. I had tears in my eyes as I accepted this responsibility and promised to rectify the issue with our competitor and anyone affected.

A few people saw my action as self-serving. The fact is that we could have just moved on and said nothing. The competitor in the end could not and would not have done anything other than get vocal about the slip our team made. But that was not the point.

I like the people at IKECA, and I like what they stand for. I like our competitors and the people who run them. The competitor is one of Omni's largest customers today, and while they are still our competitor, I teach alongside that company's leader at a KEC Training School and we will be co-presenting at the 2018 IKECA Technical Conference about the solutions our two companies bring to the market. The influence we at Omni and our competitors have on the KEC market as competent and credible people far outweighs the very slight advantage or disadvantage that may have occurred due to the mistakes we made at that show.

What really drove my fall on the sword was empathy. Our competitor's team believe in their products and so do a lot of KEC companies. For Omni to duplicate them is a testament to the quality of the solution. For Omni to belittle or defame the quality of the product to such a captive audience in the manner we did is beneath us. I had empathy for us, our competitor and their team, and our customers.

To have empathy for others and yourself shows a deeply tremendous amount of strength. To bear the emotions of others shows an intelligence that not all are endowed with. A common expression for this would be "to walk in someone else's shoes." Humans' ability to do this is astounding to me. We are able to protect, comfort, and even save others with our empathy. My hope for you is that you are an individual with the foundation to have a great amount of empathy or that you are an individual who is willing to try to build that foundation.

5.0

individualism

"*Very little is needed to make a happy life; it is all within
yourself, in your way of thinking.*" - *Marcus Aurelius*

TAKING CARE OF YOURSELF IS INDIVIDUALISM. AMERICANS are supposedly the great experiment in individualism. Our freedom is often seen as individualistic, and we are labeled selfish, egotistical, self-serving, and other names that are intended to single out our individualism. America, Individually, is amazing because of our collection of individuals mostly putting themselves first in an effort to make everyone around them better.

America is way more than a country; it is the epitome of hope. Nowhere on Earth has there ever been a place where individualism existed for the betterment of all. Take away individuals' right to speak their mind or choose their own actions and you take away the spirit of individualism that provides opportunity to every single person who seeks it. Yes, there are exceptions that have uncomfortable or even horrible outcomes. Yes, there are those who exploit the very fabric of what it is to be individual in an effort to change the definition of what it is to be. These aberrations of the true meaning of what I think individualism is in America is that same perception that is creating the generalization of what our attitude is as individuals.

Attitude

individualism is an attitude. Have you ever heard of the "American Attitude?" If the American Attitude is individualistic, then individualism is a homonym, a word that has more than one meaning. But our attitude defines us. Our attitude can be the foundation of how people perceive us.

If you have a bad attitude, your body language will be affected. I'm sure you have said to a person, "What is making you look so upset?" or "What's the matter with you?" These questions come from your view of them physically. Our attitude can affect our position at work, our position at home, and our position with friends, and most of us work to control our attitude.

Understanding your attitude is part of the self-reflection we all need to understand. How we react to situations in our life will affect both our long- and short-term attitudes. Those who, when younger, had more negative interactions and situations often grow up with attitudes that are negative or that get in the way of individual progress.

Attitude can also change moment by moment, hour by hour, day by day, month by month, or year by year. Attitude can be seasonal; *season*, of course, may be defined in ways that go beyond spring, summer, fall, or winter, as we may have a different attitude during football season or baseball season. There are even seasons associated with school; if you're a parent, a season could be the period when your kids are in or out of school.

Our ability to change our attitude is our ability to use self-reflection or experience to make changes in our attitude that can manifest themselves in our action. By changing our attitude, we can set ourselves up for success and failure.

Maturity

We learn to control things like attitude through experience or maturity. Our experience is the feedback we have that is stored in our minds about the causes and effects of our actions. If something makes us feel good, we will repeat that action, and we may find a way to repeat it better, making us feel even better. If we learn how to do something useful, we may use that experience to do it again; each time we get a little better and the experience feels better. As we mature, we begin to get better at who we are. This is not to say that who we are is necessarily good. We can get better at being bad.

Maturity is not subjective to good. A mature individual does not denote good or bad; a good or bad individual does not denote maturity. To mature in one's self is to mature in that which you have created for yourself. However, if you mature in, say, being a thief, you may be become the best thief there is and attempt more brazen thefts that lead you into punishment that is for mature criminals.

Maturity has so little to do with age; it has to do with interaction, both with self and others, and that interaction creates experience. There are also different types of maturity: emotional, physical, psychological, interpersonal. Our maturity is part of who we are, and we can use it to measure ourselves and others.

I have come across some very complex examples of maturity and immaturity. Through my travels I have been fortunate to meet some young people, under eighteen, who have more maturity than some fifty-year-olds I have met. The extent of immaturity in some among the older generations never ceases to amaze me.

One of the most notable examples in my life is a man who, through the eyes of others, has the world by the tail. He is married to an amazing woman whose own professional maturity exemplifies that of someone who has her life together. He is a brilliant business tactician and has a mind that sees things other people miss, from fine details to the most obvious. His ability to develop strategic plans is also impressive. However, his ability to see anything through is lacking. He is also amazingly self-centered and sophomoric. His maturity level is that of a sixteen-year-old; people will often see him say or do things in public that you'd expect from a teenager.

The dangers in this type of immaturity without correction is that later in life adults who exhibit such behavior are often dependent on drugs, alcohol, or other vices that lead to premature self-destruction. As peers encounter these types of people and catch on to their lack of maturity and self-control, they consciously or unconsciously avoid interaction for fear of the repercussions such a personal interaction may have.

We all have a little immaturity in us. My point in sharing the example above is that understanding maturity and the role it plays in our life is very important. Identifying traits in ourselves or in friends or family may be the observation that helps to change the path in a positive way. However, the road to maturity often is also controlled by another.

Willpower

Willpower is like fuel; it can run out. It is that inner drive that helps us get through those times when we want to quit doing what's needed to reach our goals or final objectives. If you lose your willpower, you lose that inner support, and often willpower is the only thing that keeps you going.

Because willpower is something that can run out, it can also be revitalized. For example, dieting for many is a tremendous challenge. The habits created that lead us to want or need to diet are powerful. All a diet is, is an agreement with yourself to do something different than you have been doing to affect a change in your health. With a lifestyle that would lead you down the path of dieting, it takes willpower to overcome the urge to break that diet. Changing your eating habits through diet will be a test of willpower. Cookies, cakes, donuts, pizza—regardless of what tempts you to break your diet, your ability to stay true to your diet and yourself is led by willpower.

As I've said before, multi-tasking is ineffective and inefficient. Well, tackling too many challenges in your life that tap into your willpower is another form of multi-tasking. You're draining your willpower, like you drain gas from a gas tank, when you put effort into breaking or changing habits. Just as you drain your gas tank more quickly the faster you drive, when you put effort into breaking or changing too many habits at once, it drains your willpower more quickly, thus making it more difficult for you to break one, let alone several, bad habits.

As difficult as it is to change eating habits, other habits are just as difficult—if not more difficult—to break. Eating is something that is necessary and should be the most basic and simple thing we do. Other habits aren't so simple. Smoking cigarettes isn't a necessary function for survival, but it's just as hard, if not harder, to break a smoking habit. The number of habits that take an enormous amount of willpower to overcome is infinite, and our use of willpower doesn't stop at habits. We use willpower to do other simple human functions, such as studying, which is the basis of our foundation of knowledge.

To study takes willpower. Studying is more difficult for children because they lack willpower and their immature study habits are overridden by the need to be constantly entertained. Willpower grows with each of us as we grow and mature through experience. There is no way to measure willpower; it is unique to us all. Most of the things in this book will require you to use up willpower: slowing down, self-reflection, challenging your ego, provoking thought.

When we lived in Oregon, it was a professional struggle for me. By 2005, I had been consulting for fifteen years. The role I played at IA changed dramatically when I attempted to slow down my work life and not miss my younger children's childhood as I had missed Kristin's.

My job, for all intents and purposes, from 2005 to 2008 was scheduled to be 80 percent focused on the turnaround and development of my client in Oregon. I delegated most of my other work to people in IA I trusted and began to immerse myself in the business of bowling, sports bars, and family entertainment—what a mix.

Each day I enjoyed the less than two-mile drive to work. I enjoyed seeing René, Henry, and Mary every day. At first, I even enjoyed the challenges of effecting change at the company. Change happened very quickly and success followed, which changed my role from consultant to administrator. At the same time, my clients offered me equity in the business, further changing my perspective and my responsibilities.

Willpower was the first thing to wane when I became an administrator instead of a consultant. It took all my willpower just to get through a day at work, and there were consequences. During those first three years, I gained a lot of weight and drank more. Using up my willpower just to get through my workday left me with no willpower to maintain those other things in my life that required it: diet and exercise.

The funny thing about willpower and its effect is that it can be regained quickly. Circumstances, choices, and action can change how willpower works in your life; sometimes you won't even notice it.

About the time my first three-year contract was coming up for renewal, we opened our new hotel. Back in 2006, as a consultant and before my willpower ran out, my Oregon clients contracted me to conduct a feasibility study about building a hotel adjacent to the family entertainment center, and it was feasible. Fast-forward to the day my clients (now partners) decided they wanted to actually build the hotel. They looked at me and said, "Well since you recommended we do this as a consultant, now that you're our partner, you're in, right?" And that's how fast I became a hotel owner and manager.

The hotel renewed my role as a consultant for a while. As we built and then opened the hotel, the challenges were such that it required no willpower for me to go to work. The funny thing is that at the same time I lost weight, worked out again, and slowed down my partying; the willpower to battle those demons was available again.

I have been able to track this roller coaster ride of willpower through my life. I know what things in my life take the most willpower. When my life is challenged too much too fast, and my willpower wanes, the first things to be affected are the things that are easy to give up on and I tend to lose the willpower to overcome them. It's easy for us all to fall back into a comfortable focus and allow these things to take over: drinking, weight gain, smoking.

If you slow down and think about those things that test your patience or challenge your ability to pay attention, you will find that those are the things that use up your willpower. To succeed in those things that challenge you most, you will need to measure and control your willpower. If you can find a way to develop new habits that remove the need for willpower, you have a better chance at reaching your goals and objectives.

Goals

As I sit here contemplating exactly what I want to convey about goals, I realize that almost every self-help author brings this particular issue into their lesson. I don't want to tell people how to set and achieve goals; I think that ability is very personal. You may say, "I don't know how to set a goal and know less about how to reach a goal." A goal is like a target, but without willpower and being honest with yourself, you will struggle with goal setting and goal achievement.

To hit a target consistently, you need practice. The best way to train yourself to be a goal setter and achiever is to practice goal setting and achievement with things that are easily achievable. I like the analogy of connect the dots. Connect the dots was created to teach children how to draw and follow direction. Learning how to set and achieve goals can be just as simple. You need to establish your goal and make it as realistic and simple as possible. The goal you set is not important; this is your practice.

Next, think about and outline the steps needed to reach your goal. We will use the weight loss analogy here.

I struggle with being happy with my weight. I carry an average walking weight of about 225; I can get as heavy as 235 and as light as 220. I have been carrying this range of weight since 2010, and before that I carried it from 2007 to about 2009. In 2009, however, I was able to drop my weight to 205 using a connect-the-dots application of goal setting.

My target weight was 205, and I started at 236. I decided to try to lose thirty-one pounds in twelve weeks—a short time. I wrote down my goal and looked at the things that affected my ability to stay on target (the things that tapped into my willpower). The biggest issue was consistent weight fluctuations. Due to this issue, one of my "dots" was to weigh in at the same time on the same days each week: Tuesday and Saturday.

My next issue was eating. I needed to track what I was eating to ensure that I could identify the proper foods and nutrition I needed as well as stay on target. I bought a mini-calendar and logged my food intake there. It was easy for me because I was doing the Atkins diet; today it's also known as the Keto diet. My "dot" for eating was not eating carbs each day. Each dot served as a kind-of mini-goal.

By breaking up the ultimate goal of losing thirty-one pounds into twelve weeks, I was able to track my progress consistently and see the results. This is the measure part of goal setting. When you are losing weight, at times it's very difficult to sense that you're actually losing weight. As with any goal, if you cannot measure it you cannot control it, and you must stay in control of your goals. If you make measuring your goal part of your routine, your goal and the "dots" (or objectives) you have set will always be your top priority. This ensures that you have a better chance of achieving your goals.

The ability to focus on your goal and the smaller tasks needed to reach them is what I equate to being intentional. You must be intentional about your goals; set your intentions and then act on them.

You can set goals for just about anything and use them to achieve those things in your life that you deem important. It does not matter what the goal is: to lose weight, make money, get a job. The important thing about your goal is that you slow down, write down the goal, and then write what is needed to reach that goal. Everything that is needed to reach your goal is a "dot" in your personal connect-the-dots picture. If a dot requires additional effort to achieve, divide that into smaller attainable actions (dots) that you can reach. If you find that reaching your goal within the original time frame is not feasible, consider adjusting your time frame. All goals can be reached with time.

Goal setting often fails because of unrealistic expectations. Life is complicated, and you still have an obligation to live your life and take care of your responsibilities. Adding tasks to your life can be difficult; give yourself a break and set realistic goals. For some, it may be difficult to complete goals due to the experience of failing to reach that goal in the past. Failure is never a reason to give up on yourself or your goals.

Failure

I am always disheartened when I see people give in to the notion that failure is the end. Failure is the beginning. Failure is where opportunity finds us. Success is almost always bred out of some sort of failure.

There are an infinite number of examples of people whose failure was the catalyst of amazing outcomes. Henry Ford, Walt Disney, Bill Gates, Michael Jordan, me, and you! Let's begin with some famously successful people who were failures.

"Failure is simply the opportunity to begin again, this time more intelligently." - Henry Ford

Henry Ford was a failed machinist who had garnered no respect for his work. Ford had a dream, and his tenacity to be better and his ability to self-reflect and listen to others in the face of almost continuous failure paid off in what we know today as one of the largest companies in the world.

Failures can often be rooted in perception, both of others and of ourselves. Ford overcame a lack of respect for his ideas in a time when communicating to the masses was more about personal one-on-one influence and not about mass communication. Ford used his ability to personally listen to the issues holding him back. He had the tenacity to pick himself up regardless of the challenge or setback, from dismissal by investors and consumers to failure of his products around the country.

Despite each setback or failure, Ford reflected on his position and pushed forward. He was grounded in who he was as a person and knew the technology he was trying to bring to the market. Failure can be used to focus us; it inherently causes us to slow down, take that next step, reflect, plan, be deliberate, and try again. When you use the tools we discuss here in the face of failure, failure becomes a tool to move forward, not an option or excuse to stop and give up.

"The difference in winning and losing is most often not quitting." - *Walt Disney*

Walt Disney was fired for not being creative. For us today it's hard to imagine a man like Walt Disney being terminated for his lack of creativity. However, one of his first enterprises, Laugh-O-Gram Studio, went bankrupt. There are a number of stories of amazingly successful people who have overcome the failure of bankruptcy and gone on to be wildly successful. Walt Disney was turned down over 300 times seeking financing his ideas. Failure is another example where we use our willpower to align our goals and strive for what we believe in. Walt Disney believed in his vision for what his ideas would bring to the market, and his ability to self-reflect, improvise, and stay the course has provided joy for billions of people.

"Reward worthy failure—experimentation." - Bill Gates

Bill Gates dropped out of Harvard University.

"I've missed more than 9000 shots in my career. I've lost almost 300 games. 26 times, I've been trusted to take the game winning shot and missed. I've failed over and over and over again in my life. And that is why I succeed."
- Michael Jordon

Michael Jordan did not make his high school varsity basketball team. Chris Archer and Mark Buehrle are two of many MLB players who did not make their high school baseball team. The best baseball players in the world have batting averages in the range of .325 to .350; that means they fail 65–70 percent of the time.

Failure has a way of leading us to where we need to go. Failure is not discriminatory in that it is felt at one time or another by every human on Earth. With the right mindset, failure will become a power tool in your life. Failure—when seen through maturity or experience and handled with the right attitude—will surely lead to prosperity.

Prosperity

Prosperity is the positive culmination of all we do. Prosperity is the state in which we feel that all is right in our world, when we are not searching or reaching for something more to make us content. Prosperity is not always a product of wealth, status, acceptance, or image; prosperity is individual to each of us and can only be defined individually.

If I were to ask most people, "Do you think *insert name of famous person from tabloid here* is prosperous?" the answer would likely be yes. However, fame and fortune do not always equal prosperity. Most of what we read is about relationship failure, suicide, drug addiction, bad behavior, and, quite frankly, lives that appear to be anything but prosperous.

What makes you happy will make you prosperous. I meet people every day who embrace the life they are given. Many of these people are factory workers, office workers, first responders, and trade workers. Most do not make great sums of money; many struggle financially. All have some sort of work-life balance and have friends, family, or both involved at some level in their lives. All are comfortable with their station; though many are working to learn and grow beyond it, some just like the simplicity or regularity of what they do. All are content with who they are, and when you meet them you can't help but feel their positive energy and contentment with life.

I think of one client in Southern California in particular. His business was diesel truck repair, and he had an amazing location in the Valley, just outside Los Angeles. His shop could handle eight trucks at once and had plenty of space for any size truck. There was also room outside for trucks to park and some space for work to be done outside. The company was family owned and had been in business for more than thirty-five years.

When I was referred to this client, the business was losing money, horribly. The company had lost direction and struggled to define itself, not easy to do for a diesel repair shop. The shop was disorganized, the money was day-to-day, and the employees were both disorganized and day-to-day. Annual sales were well into seven figures, and at the time the owner had reinvested almost one million dollars in losses and capital expenditures, much of it borrowed against the property.

When I first sat down with this owner, it was very clear he was unhappy. I was ushered into what I thought was a lavish office for a diesel repair shop. The office overlooked the work area and was upstairs above the front counter and customer waiting area. The owner was dressed in what can only be called Southern California Preppy. As we began to talk about his business, he kept referring to wishing he could just "turn a wrench" again. He explained his struggles with keeping pace with growth, regulation, changing technology, and money. We shared stories about employee and customer service issues he faced, seemingly on a regular basis.

We also talked about his home life. He lived beyond his means, which pushed him to perform better at work or grow the business. He talked about his "friends," who to me seemed to be other business owners or professionals who worked in less hands-on positions: white-collar types. After our back and forth, I asked him one question: "What makes you happy?"

He answered that less stress and an ability to see his family regularly would make him happy and that he really liked working on trucks. I did not have him elaborate on his family or the stress, I already knew intuitively what those answers meant, but I did ask him to explain in more depth why he liked working on trucks.

His answer was typical of the people I interview during our BizVision process; the whole experience of working on trucks made him happy. The challenges of solving the problem is what he enjoyed most at work, which for trucks he was good at. He liked communicating with truck drivers and other mechanics, both to resolve issues and the life stories they share in between truck repair and maintenance. Being on the floor with his team, immersed in his business, was what he was all about; he felt fulfilled from the new experiences each day brought him.

I asked my next question: "Why did you ever leave that job?" He looked at me and said, "I didn't, I just became the boss."

Becoming the boss does not imply taking yourself from what you love and turning yourself into some bureaucratic zombie who fits some stereotypical role created by those who have little to no understanding about what makes companies prosperous.

I told my client to take a vacation. He had contracted with us to fix this issue and could trust that in our work with his bank and attorneys, day-to-day issues would be resolved. He took off one week. We spent the week going about fixing his company. It was a simple one-two punch of decisions; we developed a chief operations officer (COO) position and we refurbished the owner's garage area.

The client came back maintaining his status as president of his company. We first showed him his new work area: one of the garage stalls easily seen from his office. We showed him a work schedule that allotted 60 percent of his time to turning wrenches. We introduced him to what a COO position could provide to him and how with proper business tools he could trust what was happening in the office and with his company while he worked with his team shoulder to shoulder.

Today, that company is one of the largest private truck repair facilities in Southern California. The owner still turns a wrench, though now he spends more time with his family, which for him is his prosperity. Prosperity is about your individual level of balance. If you are pursuing happiness and that happiness is defined by something or someone else and is not a definition individual to you, you will not find happiness, and prosperity will escape you.

6.0

Communication

*"Whatever words we utter should be chosen with care for people will
hear them and be influenced by them for good or ill." – Buddha*

COMMUNICATION IS THE KEY TO SUCCESS IN ALMOST ALL situations. Most personal conflict is the result of a lack of or misunderstanding in communication. How we communicate matters. From the words we say, to the words we write, to the inflection or tone of our voice and our body language, communication is powerful.

Some of the most followed and revered people on Earth were able to gain so many supporters because of their impeccable ability to communicate. Humans will follow other humans into great glory or great misery on a leader's singular ability to instill courage and conviction through communication. Whole societies are influenced by communication, dividing or bringing together entire countries. Repetitive communication, regardless of truth, can be perceived as reality and can alter history forever.

When I think of that last statement, I am reminded of some of the history lessons and people we celebrate and despise. Through his own oratory and his regime's propaganda, Adolf Hitler encouraged an entire nation and more to get behind fascism and all that it stands for. His influence on his and other societies had people doing and accepting atrocities that are clearly abhorrent to common society. Right alongside Hitler are people like Josef Stalin and Mao Zedong, who promoted communism with communication.

On the positive side are individuals such as Abraham Lincoln, whose eloquence and inspiring message about freedom led to the abolition of slavery. In the twentieth century, Martin Luther King, Jr., carried on in that spirit. Think about what motivational speakers such as Tony Robbins have done for countless people through influence and teachings, all through communication.

People follow those who can communicate well. Men died for George Patton, because they believed in what the general communicated. He instilled bravery and alleviated fear to the point where men ran in to certain death to preserve freedom for people an ocean away. To be a great communicator takes more than an ability to just say words. It takes a passion for what you believe is right or wrong. That passion can be transferred to others, through words and action.

For me, communication is a skill I must work at every day. I am not a great orator, and I do not think of myself as a great writer. However, I like to speak and love to write. I have, since 1990, relied on either René or Mary to edit my public writing. Through the years, I have certainly improved; their edits have decreased, and my words have become more thoughtful. I wrote my first book before meeting René back in the late 1980s, when I met Jack Danger (whom I have previously mentioned as a major influence on who I am today). One of the things Jack taught me was how to prepay a mortgage. He instructed me in how to use the amortization schedule to pay off a mortgage early and how to calculate the return on investment (ROI).

I applied that basic knowledge, coupled with a lot of ignorance and even less ability to write, in writing a booklet explaining this program in a structured way. I then came up with the idea to hold seminars in restaurants where for $75 a person could come get a meal and learn how to apply the teachings in my booklet to their personal mortgages. Unfortunately, it was an amazing failure.

I think that maybe twelve people showed up at a restaurant called the Wagon Yard in Northern Phoenix, Arizona, three being my uncle, father, and stepmother. I had printed a few hundred books, but after that disappointing beginning I set that project aside for more fruitful work like installing computerized accounting systems.

Fast-forward to 1990, when I met René. She edited the original booklet, and through the randomness of life I met a guy who was also in the prepaid mortgage business. I resurrected this literary work of art and once again set out to sell the program. This time I sold it for $29.95 in bulk via mail order ads in magazines and newspapers. I even convinced someone to go out and sell this program to people door to door. I think I sold another twelve (really, a few more than twelve, but not many more).

In the end, I sold the entire program to a company that did mortgage acceleration work; they took it and made it marketable. The lesson for me, however, was that communication is powerful. I'm not sure I thought this consciously at the time, but at some point I realized that my original work of writing had value to people. My style of writing was the catalyst for someone else to take what I started and turn it into something marketable. My ability to identify an issue and communicate solutions had value.

I expanded upon this style of communication, and it is now what I use for submitting proposals to our potential clients. This concept that proposals can teach a lesson about a potential client's possibilities appealed to our target audience because of my unique style of communicating.

Communication built our first company. Communication also expanded my insight into other opportunities. The overall scope of our entire organization is built on the foundation of communication. We begin all projects by learning about our clients and how they communicate; it is from this original understanding that we help our clients affect change to reach their goals. My journey to learn the full value of communication was not complete until 1994, but it was in 1991 that I began to learn the value of self-communication.

It was during the early years that my deeper understanding of organizational continuity would begin to affect my work. From 1991 to 1994, we would identify the deficiencies in our clients' companies and then develop a systemized solution. This was when PC-based accounting systems were just beginning to be widely adopted and conveying the advantages of these systems was at first a struggle. This period marked the beginning of the communication transition from written and spoken word to electronic communications.

One of my early ERP implementations was for a company that managed documents and sold document management equipment. This company had a robust digital records conversion business where they would scan documents onto either microfiche or what at the time was new electronic savings to hard drives. This company's early migration projects from paper to digital platforms gave me an early look at the future of communication. Back then there was a sense that the world could and would go paperless, but, as we have learned, this has yet to happen. However, what we have done is change how quickly and efficiently every individual person and Individual company can communicate to the masses.

During this time, I was learning about how local area networks were becoming more robust and allowing better collaborative communications within the smallest of businesses. We had to develop a way to quickly introduce these advantages to potential users. Our method involved designing and using lessons. To build my skill, I read a lot of books about presentations and writing, but I also decided that writing and speaking were very different. When we write, it is much harder to convey our true emotion and passion than when we speak.

From 1991 to 1995, we still did most of our communicating via written and verbal exchanges, and the written word was delivered via paper. We became proficient in writing these outlines and still use the same format today.

In 1995, AOL became a very prominent player in business communications. The ability to communicate via media that could deliver written information instantly dramatically changed our approach toward communication; we did not know how dramatic this change would be. Our ability to influence the market went from costly to less costly. The access we had to our target audience was opened up.

At our disposal, we also had a new way to teach our clients how to communicate. Leaders could immediately deliver messages to individuals or an entire organization with a single click. Managers could be updated on progress as it happened, without having to speak to anyone. Documents could be shared electronically, in real time, from desktop to desktop.

The entire dynamic of how we communicate was being turned on its head. As email took off, technology improved to where it is today. We can send a note to anyone on the planet from our phone and it can be read almost instantly. We can send documents, conduct research, and affect change with our communication in seconds.

Self-Communication

Looking in the mirror is what I call self-communication. The first step to being honest is to be honest with yourself. Although I am sometimes guilty of this, it never ceases to amaze me the number of people who lie to themselves. Our main goal here is to proactively recognize the lies we tell ourselves and then correct them to enhance our self-communication skills.

Self-communication cannot be done properly when the communication is false. Imagine trying to design a product while your partner constantly lies to you about the budget. Would you be able to trust anything your partner said? Imagine all the time lost developing this product because of this ineffective communication. If lying cannot serve as the basis for effective communication in a team setting, then it certainly cannot work for self-communication.

We do things in life that we know are destructive, and we tell ourselves that doing so is okay if it does not affect others, or we justify a destructive act by telling ourselves the effect is not "bad." But what is the effect on you? Shouldn't you protect yourself from any destructive behavior? I was in a board meeting recently where I heard a board member justify violating a noncompete clause. The justification was that within the confines of the board meeting, the violation was justified because the company we were violating had issues with us and those issues justified our actions. At the time, there was an open discussion using information from the person who caused us to violate the noncompete. The discussion was led by the board member who had justified the violation and another who bought into the reason. It did not take long for one of the other members to challenge the board about this violation; the silence after that admonishment was palpable.

This is highly destructive behavior. The member who violated the noncompete, when challenged, finally admitted that the justification was a cover for not doing what was right. The fact that one board member would confront the other is a good example of going beyond self-communication; if you're in a meeting and telling yourself that what you are hearing or reading is wrong, but you continue to allow it to go unchallenged, you become part of the dishonesty.

The consequences for this violation were nonexistent for the organization but quite high for the member who justified it. There have been a number of conversations between peers on the board that question the integrity of the members who justified a contractual violation. These questions may hurt the integrity of the overall board, as an undercurrent of distrust now exists among the members.

Our actions have consequences, regardless of who we think our actions affect or do not affect. All actions have a reaction. Life is like a pinball game of action and reaction, constantly bouncing through time. How honest we are about our actions and reactions is the key to understanding ourselves as an individual. This honesty comes from within and expands outward to your sphere of influence.

Being honest with yourself is generally hindered by fear. For some, it can be fearful to look within and to truly know one's self, but with self-communication you must let go of that fear. Who should know you better than you know yourself? We often fear that honesty will hurt, be hard to deal with, or elicit a negative reaction from an outside source. It's difficult to go beyond that emotion of fear and realize the overall effect that a lack of honesty will have on us and our community.

One of the best ways to tackle self-deception is to write or journal your challenges. Each time I feel challenged to be honest or need help making a decision, I write the issues down and then read about it as if I am a third party. I have found that looking at my decision-making process like an outsider has helped me to peek into my overall decision-making process. What this process has revealed scared the hell out of me.

I noticed how irrational I could be with certain decisions and/or choices. If I had a strong emotional tie or there was some perceived gain (emotional, financial, or both), I could quickly skip over key issues that may or may not have altered my decision. As I continued to develop my ability to self-communicate, I noticed that my decisions became more thoughtful and that my propensity to fool myself was reduced. However, regarding very individual or personal decisions, I will note that I can still fool myself.

When thinking about how you might begin communicating with yourself, I recommend above all else writing. Unlike when you write to others, you will know the emotion that fueled your own writing. You will have context behind the words you write and read. I send myself texts or emails as a reminder to do something. The written word provides for us all the opportunity to release, privately if we wish, the emotions that build up in our lives in a healthy way. If you find a way to slow yourself down by journaling, try to view your journal entries from a third-party perspective. Acting as though you are another person who does not have your background or basis for knowledge will help you to highlight flaws.

When you begin to communicate more honestly with yourself, you will notice that you communicate with others more clearly. One of the biggest challenges when communicating with others is that others do not have the benefit of knowing your internal thought process. This missing context means they do not always know which direction you may be coming from when communicating.

For example, sometimes I already know how certain aspects of a particular recommendation will affect my target audience before I make the recommendation. Unfortunately, this means that I may begin discussing the benefit before I've laid the foundation, and anyone who does not have the proper context is unprepared to hear my communication. When I begin a communication, I have the benefit of information and knowing the entirety of the story, but I must always remember that my audience does not necessarily know what I know or have the same perception; this is why context matters.

Context is that part of communication that, when misused, can alter your future. I was recently involved in an ERP project where a manager did not want to take responsibility for his actions. To skirt responsibility, he would take pieces of emails and string them together to create a narrative that removed his responsibility from the situation and diverted the focus to others. This high-level manager would do this often, both in writing and verbally. This is how salespeople and journalists—professions that are typically celebrated for above average communication skills—can really cause havoc in the world.

When you miscommunicate issues out of context, the decisions made going forward will be flawed. For example, in the instance with the ERP system, we had some underlying contractual obligations that were not conveyed in detail. The managers took parts of the contract and used only those parts to communicate with their team, giving their team a false understanding of the contract terms—leading them to believe that the terms were changeable. The terms of the contract, however, were not able to be altered. The contract had specific terms that were agreed to, and those terms negated a number of solutions that were being considered.

These issues are rooted in self-communication. At some point, these people had to consider the truth as they used context to disrupt the programs in place that were contributing to the company's more viable future. I cannot count the number of projects that I have been asked to join that went bad due to a person or persons taking facts out of context and making them work to their advantage, not to their customers' or constituents' advantage. Sometimes this is unintentional; sometimes it is not. The unintentional issues could almost always have been resolved or avoided had the originators reviewed with their self the issues from a more objective mindset.

It's necessary for self-communication to be truthful for it to benefit you. If you find yourself in the company of those who like to twist words and construct a misleading narrative, you will find that keeping documentation of events will help you tremendously.

Written Word

In 1992, I found myself working with a company that audited utility bills for large companies. My former company, Business Accounting Solutions (BAS), was contracted to install computers and software and manage the implementation of systems that would manage document workflow more efficiently. I was then offered an opportunity to invest in this client's company; it would prove to be prophetic, as it laid the foundation for our current business structure.

This company was very successful at the time. I was a couple years into building my company in Denver and the opportunities for me, my family, and our company were tremendous. But, as do many private partnerships with many investors, we ran into problems early. I was twenty-six and eager. I borrowed money from my mother-in-law to fill my financial needs for this contract and investment.

As a result of my youthful eagerness, I found myself as the president of this company. The company found itself in the middle of a legal action with independent contractors and vendors, and my new status of president trapped me in the middle. I was in way over my head; I found myself in meetings with shareholders I had never met and never knew were even involved in the company. My days consisted of nonstop phone calls and back-to-back meetings.

How I became president was a case of being in the wrong place at the right time. I had been calling the offices of this company every day to get paid; the company owed BAS about $240,000 and owed the other vendors about the same. BAS had supplied most of the equipment, software, and installation. As a shareholder now, I was getting a little upset, having just borrowed $15,000 from my mother-in-law. I wanted this to be a good first private external investment for us.

For about a week I called twice a day trying to reach the, then, president or vice president. I would get a receptionist who answered with the company name and acted as if she was an employee.

Finally, I got tired of calling and getting no calls back. I drove to the office, which was on the tenth floor of a twelve-story building in Aurora, Colorado. When I got to the office, it was locked. At this time, I had a cell phone but reception was spotty, so I walked down the hall and asked if I could use the phone. I called the company, and to my surprise the receptionist answered. When I told her that the doors were locked, she explained she was an answering service in downtown Denver.

Things moved quickly after that. The building manager agreed to open the door because, as we found out later, he had not heard from his tenant and the rent had not been paid. When we opened the door, the office was empty: nothing.

The founders who originally brought me into the organization all disappeared, along with the majority of the assets we sold to them. The missing assets had a value of over half a million dollars. Some of the missing assets included computer systems and software provided to the auditors and a full document management system that scanned the client documents and put them on CD-ROM—a huge step forward in early 1990s technology. I was mildly freaking out, standing in that office like a deer in the headlights.

One of our vendors had a relationship with a very good law firm. The vendor's wife was an associate at the firm and introduced me to the senior partner. When I sat with him for my first meeting and recounted the past six weeks of business with this company, he gave me one piece of advice that stuck: Always follow up a conversation that can affect you with a written note. He explained that the note should review the conversation and ask for immediate clarification if anything in your written note is inconsistent.

He then went on to explain the value of this practice. He had been through a nasty divorce recently. He had adopted the act of sending a written note whenever he had a conversation that included agreements, promises, or decisions by either party. During one conversation with his ex-wife, they had agreed to an amicable split of certain debt. His attorney followed up that conversation with a letter to his ex-wife and one to the lender that detailed the conversation and agreement. Neither the lender nor his ex-wife responded to his letter.

Later, during the final divorce proceedings, his ex-wife and the lender both wanted him to pay the full debt. He told them that he and his soon-to-be ex-wife had agreed to different terms, and both his ex-wife and the lender challenged him for proof, to which he responded by providing a copy of both letters he had sent to them in review of the original discussion. The judge ruled that he did not have to pay the debt in full.

In the end, it would be the written word that helped us all. We got control of the company with the corporate documents we had; the original shareholders and officers were all gone. We involved the local police, who at first were less than helpful, saying it was a civil issue over which they had no jurisdiction. We managed to salvage a few of the contracts the independent contractors had signed, but that only prolonged the death of the company. The company eventually just ceased to operate, leaving me with almost a quarter-million dollars of debt.

The end to this story is actually good and bad. The documents and agreements we would be able to salvage through public filings and legal actions finally showed that none of the remaining shareholders were involved. I worked out a payment agreement with the original equipment vendors. Almost two years later, I received a call from the FBI. The original vice president had been found dead in Ohio, and in the same town they found cash and computers in a storage bin; those assets were distributed to the victims of the theft. I learned that the written word had influence. Written word has more power than the spoken word because it has legal permanence.

As is apparent, I like to write. I journal on a regular basis and have since about 1996. There is no true structure to my journaling, other than that I use either a spiral bound notebook, composition journal, or Word document. I am inconsistent, and I generally don't worry about spelling, context, political correctness, or any other limitations. I journal for me and for me only. If my personal writings were ever read by third parties, I am sure that many people would find them quite upsetting—as I am sure most personal writing is.

There are dangers in the written word. Writing can lack emotion if not expressed properly, and as such can cause readers to experience emotions that were unintended by the writer toward the original sentiment. Emotion makes the written word powerful. Books have been disseminating knowledge to humans for millennia and will continue to do so for many more.

Writing provides me the support I need to take action. It creates the ingrained memory and trigger I need to spur me into action and complete the task I agreed to finish. With writing, I have the foundation to remember tasks much more easily (as I have previously discussed during accountability). There is a rule at IA: Never just tell Brian something, send it to him in written format so he won't forget.

For me, it makes information concrete and creates a sense of urgency. The written word, when used properly, can also bring a sense of closure. Why else do we put signature to paper when agreeing to thirty-year mortgages or lifetime marriages? Our written signature binds us individually/ Individually to the words on the page.

Using individualism for Individualism: The Ultimate Oxymoron

"Individual commitment to a group effort—that is what makes a team work, a company work, a society work, a civilization work." - Vince Lombardi

BEING GREAT FOR YOURSELF FIRST SO YOU CAN BE GREAT FOR others may appear selfish to some. There are dangers in teaching people to put themselves first. People will take advantage of others. People will exaggerate the concept and benefit themselves at the expense of others. In order to be the best, you must have the best to work with; this philosophy implies that if you take the best for yourself, you are leaving others with the mediocre or worst. I don't believe this is true.

First, the best for me is not the same as the best for someone else; it's entirely subjective. Expectation and perception alter the definition of a great many things; to say something is the best for you doesn't mean that it is also the best for someone else. When people's realities are different, they need different things to succeed. When you think of being the best, it is in the context of your own ability. For example, we see people say they are the best plumber in town. What does this mean? Is it because they have more experience in plumbing? Is it because they have more employees? Is it because they have the lowest prices?

Understanding who you are in all you do is vital on the quest to improve yourself for your sphere of influence. Defining what the best is for you is an important challenge that I hope you will tackle. When you realize what your best is and are able to achieve that, you will fully understand what it means to influence others positively. Finding your best means finding what your individual advantages are

We once had this amazing salesman; he was one of the best that IA has had the pleasure of employing. He had this knack of connecting with people, and he took the time to understand what he was selling; while he worked for us, he sold IT services.

Our technology company, System Design Consultants (SDC), was founded in 1997. Our IT salesman was the driving force behind our going from startup to over $2 million dollars in annual revenue. One day, he walked into the office and said he wanted to be our Vice President of Sales and laid out what he thought that position would look like. Now, at this time we had about five or six consultants, plus myself and one administrative person; we were a small company. This individual wanted a six-figure salary, a car, and other perks that are often seen in large corporations. He wanted an office and expense report.

To put his personality into context, I'll give you a little backstory. When he was hired, we decided to invite him over to our house for dinner. This house was our first Thornton home and had been built in the 1970s. We remodeled it ourselves, so it was a modest 1,887-square-foot triplex. René and I owed about $70,000 on this house, so our mortgage was very small in comparison with our peers' mortgages at the time. When he and his wife arrived at our home, we talked about the company and our goals. Then he looked around our home with his wife and said, "Well, those are great plans because it's obvious up to now you're no Rockefeller."

He then proceeded to counter propose me on some multi-level marketing program he did on the side. He was very persuasive and was obviously fixated on very material things in his personal goals; I wanted him on my team. Anyone that fixated on money who would go to almost any professional lengths to afford pretentious stuff with an ability to talk as eloquently as he could would make a great asset to our new IT company.

Back to his demand to be VP of Sales. We told him no on a VP title, but offered some other fancy-sounding title. We explained the value of the position and how successful it would be for him and our company. We explained that his success stemmed from his natural sales ability and that we needed him to sell. We were not in a position to hire another person in an administrative role, which was what he really wanted.

On his 358th day of work, seven days shy of his one-year anniversary, he walked in and quit. He informed us that he had been hired as the VP of Sales for a new startup IT company in Boulder. He went on to tell us that in his new position he would get a $60,000 salary, commissions, and a new Lexus. Now, his base with us was $24,000 a year plus a nice commission. He had made no less than $15,000 a month for the past five months. He was also sitting on project work that would make him even more money in the next year. However, since he had not worked for the company for a full year, he was not yet vested.

Five weeks later, he returned to the office and asked for his commissions. We paid his final check in full for all he earned up to his 358th day. We explained that he quit his job seven days ahead of his vesting, so he forfeited $35,000 in commissions. Boy, was he pissed. So much so, in fact, that he publicly called our senior administrator a "fat fucker" there in our offices.

Over the next few weeks we were targeted with threats and more derogatory comments, and then all went quiet. On a Monday, about six weeks later, he walked in asking me for his job back on the terms we originally gave him. I said no.

Greed, ego, and self-importance can be good or bad. This individual was an amazing salesman. However, when he used his individual to be a part of our Individual company, it proved to be toxic. I gave him advice on how to develop himself to better work with a company like ours; IA was in its infancy, but I had started developing the philosophies that are here in this book.

My advice to him was this: You need to go out and focus on being the best *you* you can be so that those you influence can benefit. You cannot expect to be accepted just for what you have done or for what you will be and offer in the future. Your value in the present is that you have a natural ability to develop and keep relationships with clients. Flexing your ego on one of your best attributes is hindering your ability to work in a group setting. The failure of the company that offered you what you wanted did not provide the individual advantages needed to succeed. So, go out and refine your sales skills and learn what it means to be a leader. Come back when you think you can work as part of a team and not just for your own gain.

He did just that, and during the time he was gone we merged our company with a much larger one. He ended up coming back about eighteen months later and integrated into our team nicely. The combined revenue of the company grew to over $7 million and we had a top-notch sales leader. He stayed on for a couple years, worked with the team, and later became a successful VP of Sales.

The lesson here is to be accountable to and for yourself and those you influence. If you put the cart before the horse, the horse may get away from you.

Accountability

One of my favorite services that we offer at IA is what I call Outsourced Accountability. One of things we taught our children was that we should be held accountable for our actions; those actions include speaking as well as doing.

In our home, we are accountable for the things we do. Being accountable is not the same as consequences; this point is often misinterpreted when I am speaking to people. Just because you accept accountability for something does not necessarily mean there will be a negative consequence.

To accept accountability or be accountable for what we say and do is part of maturity. Growing up, I was not taught accountability at all. There was no understanding of the word or what it might mean to me. My actions through childhood bear out this fact and I did almost anything I wanted until I got stepparents.

Two months before the end of seventh grade I moved to California, where I got my first lesson in accountability. First, I was emotionally in chaos. My parents had divorced for the second time. I was angry from the constant moving, and I acted out a lot, but no one paid attention, so my anger went unchecked.

When I arrived in California, my family was living in a condo close to the school I would attend: Los Cerritos. This school looked like a prison compared with the schools in Illinois. I was to enter this school knowing no one. It was also a public school; my entire education at this point was in private Lutheran schools with class sizes of around twenty students. My classes in California were twice that size.

In my first week, the bullying began—just like in Illinois. By then I had reached puberty, so I now had size and my pent-up anger to use to my advantage and fight back with. After a fight, I was suspended for three days in-school and had to meet with the counselors at school. They talked to me about managing my stress and how acting out meant that I would be held accountable.

However, this first lesson did not really set in, because I still had parents who weren't in control. I was so miserable in California that I made a stink with my parents; to the chagrin of my stepparents, I was granted permission to move back to Illinois. Bill, my stepfather, thought it would be better if I adjusted and adapted instead of bouncing between homes when I was uncomfortable. Perhaps he was right.

My move back to Illinois put me right back into chaos. My father married Michele, who at this time was twenty-one, and I was thirteen. I was not allowed to go back to Immanuel Lutheran, so I went to Dundee Middle School. My stepmother, up to this point, paid about as much attention to me as my father did—she was pregnant and young. We lived in an apartment, my ninth home in thirteen years, which we shared with her father and brother.

I adapted better to public middle school in Illinois. However, after the first week of school, a teacher took me aside. I cannot recall his name, but his comments were really jarring. He asked me about my home life. I really did not understand his question, so I just told him we lived in Village Quarter with my dad, my stepmother, her father, and her brother. He then asked me if anyone had ever talked to me about hygiene.

I told him no because I still did not understand what he meant. He proceeded to tell me that I smelled and needed to take a shower. He explained to me that I was not taking good care of myself and because I was entering puberty I needed to take better care of myself, hold myself accountable. He was not mean, he was just concerned.

Conversations such as these can be acutely embarrassing, but as I look back at this moment I now realize that this was my first true lesson in accountability; now I understood what that meant. I needed to be accountable for my actions and for my body; if not, there would be consequences such as being further marginalized by the other kids. My teacher was providing outsourced accountability for me. He often asked me if I was doing better with taking care of myself. He mentioned on a number of occasions that he recognized I was showering and doing well; he also called me out if I came to school with oily hair or body odor. He even bought me deodorant.

After my brother was born, things changed because my stepmother discovered that being a mother gives you power. Through eighth grade, I had few rules, but a new one was a curfew. Before the birth of my brother, no one held me accountable for where I was, and nobody cared if I was late. Michele became much stricter and began to hold me accountable for my actions. One of the consequences she levied against me for being late was that I would be grounded one day for each minute I was late; we went from no accountability to this, without a middle ground.

In a matter of six weeks, I learned two lessons about accountability that were dramatically different, but I was learning. Through the rest of my school years almost all of my accountability came from third parties: teachers, other parents, bosses, friends, and the police.

I lasted through ninth grade with my stepmother and father. Ironically, Michele began to really try to be more of a mother figure to me during my freshman year of high school. She began to actually pay attention to what I was doing, she offered some help, and she even gave me my own bedroom so that I would feel more comfortable at home; a week later, however, I informed them that I was moving back to California.

My stepfather was a bit more involved, but he had a different way of parenting. For one thing, I had assigned chores, and if I did not finish them he grounded me. This was pretty simple stuff and more in line with what being accountable as a teen should be. However, mixed into that was some odd lessons. For example, Bill had access to movies before they came out. We often would watch a movie on VHS weeks before it was out in movie theaters. These life lessons were teaching me that if you could find a way to not get caught, you wouldn't be held accountable.

The inconsistency of my early life lessons paved the way for me to push the boundaries as a junior and senior in high school. Accountability became a game that when played by adolescent teens can quickly turn dangerous. Nefarious drugs and guns, and the violence that accompanies them, were unfamiliar to me growing up in Illinois. California was a place that would expand my relationship with them both. This toxic mix taught me more about accountability in the next two years of my life than most other lessons in my life.

I got my first job between my sophomore and junior years in high school. By this time, I had made friends and matured enough to not continue bouncing back and forth between California and Illinois if things did not go my way. I still had very little supervision. My mother and stepfather worked hard and paid inconsistent attention to me.

My first job was at Wendy's, and my wage was $3.15 per hour. It was here where I would meet my first real drug dealer. This dealer lived in a condo complex by the Wendy's where I worked in Westlake, California. He was also friends with the manager and a couple of coworkers who happened to go school with me.

My introduction to drugs was not as a user, but as a supplier. I was offered an opportunity to sell drugs to kids at my school, specifically at parties on the weekends. My actions over the next fifteen months reinforced my complete lack of understanding of accountability and consequences.

I did not do drugs until I was a senior and had already made a name for myself as a dealer. I had the perfect cover for the money I was making because I had multiple jobs. I was working at Wendy's, cleaning the office building where my mom worked, and detailing cars. I made so much money that my parents borrowed $2,000 from me to buy an MGB convertible.

As I began to use drugs, my life changed. People held me accountable for the things I was doing: not completing homework and ditching school. This would culminate in my being given a choice to either go to jail or go into the military; the ultimate place to learn about accountability.

One day after a rather hectic night of partying, I left drugs in my mother's car. By this time, my parents knew that I was doing drugs, but they had not realized the extent of my drug use. When my mother found the drugs in her car, she did what she should have done; she turned the drugs in to the police. This did not affect me legally right away. The police did, however, have me on their radar; I was also on the radar of the person whose drugs had been turned in. They were not paid for and were in my possession to sell for the dealer.

The dealer was not happy. The drugs were worth a lot of money, and since the cops had them, I could not sell them to repay him. My parents kicked me out of the house, and I was living with friends, though my parents let me come and go during the day to a certain extent.

One weekend when my parents were out of town, the house was robbed. During the burglary, a lot of things were taken, including guns, jewelry, stereo equipment that both my parents and I owned, and my computer (a Commodore 64). My parents called the police and then told me; I had a feeling I knew who had done it.

I went to the drug dealer and told him I would make up the difference, but I needed him to get my parents' stuff back. After some negotiations, we came to an agreement and I was told where to go and get the stuff. My girlfriend at the time went with me. We put everything into her car and took it back to my parents' house.

When we arrived, I was met by my parents and the police. Included in the stolen property from our house was one added item, the gun I had been carrying around with me. The police put me under arrest for possession of stolen property—my own property and that of my parents.

I was taken to jail, booked, then taken down to county jail in Ventura, California. On day two, I was visited by the police again; this time they expanded my charges. The gun I had with me had been stolen from Oklahoma. I had never even been to Oklahoma at that time in my life and did not even really know where it was. So now I had possession of stolen property and possession of a stolen firearm.

On day five, my girlfriend's family put their house up for my bail and I bonded out. I was given a public defender; my parents essentially disowned me. It was during the negotiation process that I would learn of my choice: military or jail. The military option ensured that the charges would be expunged at some time in the future and would not follow me; accountability became a real thing for me.

Since that time, I have been faced with other decisions that required accountability, except now that equation is something I consciously consider with each action. The lesson through all of this is that we all can use help holding ourselves and others accountable. Lack of accountability is not a good thing. If we go through life and allow ourselves and others to escape accountability, then we instill habits that can prove to be amazingly destructive to our future.

For example, if we are not held accountable for being late, we may miss opportunities or be labeled as unreliable. If we are not held accountable for our promises, we may be labeled untrustworthy. If we don't hold our children accountable, they may mature into adults who won't themselves be accountable or teach accountability to those they influence.

Being accountable is not negative. If we agree to something then we should expect to be held accountable; if you agree to something without this expectation, then you're a liar. Nobody wants to be known as a liar. If you act upon holding people accountable and they fight back, stop and ask them if they would rather you hold them accountable or if they would rather be known as a liar. The act of holding someone accountable in this manner is not negative, it's a positive lesson.

If accepting your consequences is more tolerable than fulfilling that for which you are being held accountable, then you will be held accountable for the choice you make to accept those consequences. When I know that I cannot hold myself accountable for something, I solicit help from family, friends, and employees. Exceptions surround every lesson; I do all I can to make sure that I hold myself accountable so that I am consistent in following through with my obligations.

If you are consistent in holding those you influence accountable, you will reinforce that accountability is a positive thing. This in turn will produce people who are more accountable. Being consistent, in all things, is the optimum way to gain the results you want. When I am journaling my solutions to issues, I will often look back on other decisions to ensure consistency. I know that if I am inconsistent, there may be a consequence that factors into my accountability.

Consistency

We've now learned about self-reflection and how deep our understanding needs to be in order to influence others effectively. Our consistency or lack of consistency is something that offers us opportunity and advantage. How we use our understanding of consistency and commingle that with accountability can be one of the most powerful lessons in this book.

In our business, we use tools to help us commingle these two powerful human actions. Accountability and consistency combined are purely human traits, meaning that humans can control the application of both to effect change in dramatic ways.

We use project management tools to map our projects. In our projects, we employ tasks that lead us to milestones. These milestones are a snapshot and measurement of the overall progress of our project, and we use these in combination to make us consistent and provide accountability for our team. When we combine the consistent use of our project management system across all the affected people, we are almost certain to reach our goals. When individuals collaborate using the same tool (consistency) and hold each other accountable for the work needed to reach agreed-upon milestones, the results are powerful.

My greatest value to my team and our clients is my ability to map out a project and create the plan needed to reach goals. My ability to provide outsourced accountability to those involved, while empowering them to hold themselves accountable and stay the course needed to reach our combined agreed-upon goal, is what has provided the most influence for me. My abilities have helped hundreds of thousands of people become the best they can be and amazingly resourceful and successful. The best examples I have come from my own home and my own teams.

René and I are guilty of spoiling our children; in that we have been consistent. The level of spoiling has increased from Kristin, our oldest, to Henry, our youngest. However, we have also been consistent in teaching each of our kids the value of follow-through, consistency, accountability, and consequences. In the early years of our parenting, I don't think we used these words, but our actions instilled the tenets within those we influenced.

We empower our children. We give them boundaries and expect them to live within those boundaries, and when they don't we hold them accountable. We teach them what accountability means, and if the consequence is acceptable, then it's their choice to make.

Kristin moved into our home as a junior in high school. The move for her was very similar to my move from Illinois to California; she moved from rural Texas to urban Colorado. Kristin adapted well to the move and immediately made friends. We tried to provide for her the guidance and foundation needed to be a good adult, the best we could do with only two years left of childhood. Kristin came to us after fifteen years of being parented by her mother and stepfather, who took an entirely different approach.

She came to us with few boundaries. She would pretty much get what she wanted. Consequences were inconsistent, but when they happened in her home back in Texas, they were loud and violent. We are not yellers. In fact, we don't fight or argue much in our family.

Kristin's first test with us was a navel piercing. Her mother and stepfather permitted this without our consent; Kristin learned a lesson. The next issue was a tattoo. We said no, but her mom and stepfather allowed it.

For us, consequences in this instance were difficult. But we knew that the act of defiance was not preparing Kristin for adulthood.

While Kristin's mom and stepfather decided to divorce, they could not offer Kristen much help. Kristin turned to the next available people: family. My recollection of accountability was outlined previously and not being able to provide this lesson to my daughter would prove to be just as damaging. Ultimately, it was fulfilling and positive, as my own experiences were and as most experiences are.

I had family members who cosigned for Kristin's new car, then turned to me to help with payments she missed. Other family members provided her with money to attend Colorado State University, where Kristin flunked out. Those family members asked me to repay them. I did not pay anyone. My family needed to be accountable for their own actions; they provided this help to Kristin and in doing so took away her ability to learn lessons but created an opportunity to learn some of their own.

Kristin eventually chose to move back to Texas, where I think she felt accountability may not be so direct and where she might receive the type of support she felt she needed. Life has a way of circling back around and teaching good lessons. The lesson for Kristin began here due to mine and René's consistency with some added effort by my mother and stepfather, Jeff, who decided that they were going to take a more vested interest in helping her grow.

When René and I did not bail out those family members who now felt we should, they stopped providing support to Kristin. Her mother could not afford it. We would provide basic support—food and shelter—if needed, but we did not reward failure with more opportunity to fail.

Kristin was shortly thereafter blessed with a daughter. She pulled herself up and with the help of tough love she put herself through school. Today she is married and is amazingly successful in a career that she loves, with a daughter who herself is beginning to teach her the lessons children often provide to parents: how to be the ones who provide accountability and consistency.

It is my impression that Kristin recognized that mine and René's actions, coupled with her upbringing, proved that making good choices will bring good rewards. Consequence of action has a way of waking people up. Once you face the consequences once or twice, consistently, the message begins to resonate. By learning that my love for her had nothing to do with my duty to hold her accountable, and that my love isn't something that could be used to reinforce poor choices, Kristin began holding herself accountable and started making good choices.

Consistency is difficult to achieve in and of itself. To use consistency to effect change is even more difficult. However, if you can embrace consistency as a helpful tool, you will see change. As with all practices, however, consistency will help you only if you are consistently doing something that is beneficial; consistently doing something that is harmful will result in undesirable consequences. Enter Henry.

Now, I'm not going to tell you Henry has grown into anything negative. Henry is amazing. But I will describe how being consistent in his life altered our lives for good and bad.

Henry used to be an amazing BMX rider. He began riding bikes without training wheels at age two and never looked back. He would entertain himself for hours just riding in circles. When we moved to Oregon, BMX offered him opportunities to improve his natural skills and us an opportunity to keep the kids busy. Henry would beg to go to the track and just ride, and René would take Mary and let him ride.

We did this for three years. We were consistent; we never missed a practice session or race in our hometown or, for that matter, anywhere in Oregon. In fact, as Henry got better and better, our immersion in the sport became a borderline obsession for both René and myself. Through it all we would drag Mary along, setting her up with games and other distractions to appease as best we could. For three years, this was our life, our choice for us and for our kids. We never asked Henry or Mary how they felt about this—we were consumed.

The consequences of this forced consistency were multi-dimensional: good, bad, and ugly.

Let's begin with the ugly. Mary would be ignored to a certain extent and turn to friends who would prove to be emotionally destructive and potentially worse. She was introduced to Drake, her first boyfriend, who was a couple of years older than Mary; he took advantage of Mary's need for attention. At the same time this was going on, our push to have Henry perform blinded us to the treatment he was getting by his BMX race team.

This would all come to a head one day when Henry said simply, "I quit." He hated riding because of the pressure, the pressure we and his team were putting on him. Henry was eight; the amount of pressure he was experiencing would have been a lot for anyone to handle, let alone an eight-year-old. We were shocked back into reality. We identified what was happening to Mary and Henry within a few months of each other. It was a sad testament to what child sports can do to a family. What seemed like consistent time together as a family was actually fueled by the emotional highs when Henry won, not by actually being together. In doing this consistently, we created this vacuum in both our children that was filled with negative issues.

In the end, this lesson about negative consistency coupled with comfortable focus and being selfish, not selfless or empathetic, provided for us as a family a renewed focus on being together. Over the next few years, we would embark on more focused family vacations. Mary went from a shy and introverted young lady to the captain of her cheer team, and today she is an amazingly successful and productive woman.

Henry, by the way, is still spoiled but with a renewed love of riding bikes, though not competitively. In fact, Henry played sports but never really embraced one in a fiercely competitive way. Even though he never fully embraced a sport, he ended up with offers to play college baseball. He instead chose a path toward his ultimate dream since age six: to be a Navy SEAL Officer. He is attending college on a naval ROTC scholarship.

Our ability to stay true to our convictions and be consistent has provided something for René and me that is far more valuable than money: Respect.

Earning Respect

Being an asshole is not how I want to be remembered by anyone. When we lived in Oregon, I felt like I needed to be an asshole and wear it as a badge of honor due to the influence that being known as one afforded me. It's interesting how others' perception of us can actually change us. I never wanted to be a person who was seen as a bad guy, but I was pushed to feel like I had to be.

It is an honor when your children respect you. Having your family, boss, coworkers, and friends respect you is the next level of feeling good for me. If you are consistent with positive aspects in your life, you will gain respect. However, respect must be earned, and that takes time. Respect is not a given; all too often I see people demand respect due to their status in life; the only place this really, truly works is in the military, where the hierarchy is so clearly defined by protocol and procedure.

Early in my own career, I learned that respect was earned. In the military, I was fortunate to be around officers and non-commissioned officers (NCOs) who understood the status of their rank, but also understood that they had a responsibility to measure up to that rank. Before I left the Army, I was at Fort Sill, Oklahoma. As I was sitting one day in the battalion offices, a lieutenant colonel walked by and noticed my 18th Airborne Corp patch and jump boots. He inquired about the patch and my current position, to which I replied that I was leaving the military and was stationed at

Fort Sill for my final 45 days. Somehow, he assigned me to him for those remaining days.

He commanded an Airborne unit that interacted a lot with artillery and was at Fort Sill often to interface with the training facilities there. Over the last 45 days of my military life, I was delegated a lot of menial tasks that supported this officer, all of them important to him. His rules were: Be there when I say, always represent the Airborne with your best, and never miss physical training (PT). He would provide for me lists of responsibilities and schedules, then go on to do whatever lieutenant colonels do. The respect he afforded me was kind of a shock, and the respect I had for him never wavered; in fact, I have done work for this man through my career, and he has helped me and my team be the great professionals we are today.

Respect can take weeks, months, or years to build, but it can be destroyed in a day. I have had my share of destructive moments too. Through my career I have had a number of business partners, none of whom are even remotely a part of our lives today. Each season with a partner has left me with an amazing lesson, and none of those lessons has left me with any animosity, jealousy, or anger; mostly, it has just left me with empathy.

Having just returned home from Oregon, where I had some of my biggest challenges when it came to respect, I still feel good about the legacy I left behind. This validation of my efforts to provide foundation and long-lasting lessons to those I influenced helps me to put into perspective the self-reflective information I take away each time I visit.

Since leaving, I have heard how well the two businesses we had are doing. I am so proud of the teams, primarily because the teams today are the same teams we put in place before we sold the companies. When I look back at companies we had partnerships with in the mid-1990s and early 2000s, I get the same satisfaction. In fact, the first five people I ever hired are still working for the companies I used to own or had tremendous influence in, and those same people are still acquaintances I hear from or reach out to on an annual basis. To have people you are not related to stay in your life despite dramatic changes in profession, personal life, and living locations is a powerfully positive feeling.

Earning respect means that you have the opportunity to control this. You can be someone who is good at holding people accountable, firm in your convictions, and still realize and celebrate being respected. Yes, you will have those who will say derogatory things about you, you may even feel derogatory emotions towards them, but the difference (for me) is that right after that initial flair of negative emotion comes immediate empathy.

When you come across people who want to live in the negative circumstances of the past, don't let their inability to move on bring you back to a place where you may damage your own self-respect or, worse, the respect of others. Slow down the emotion, reflect on what positivity may have occurred since the events that caused such animosity, and leave them—empathizing with them for their inability to do the same.

If you are a person who cannot seem to let go of the issues that are the foundation of your negative feelings and emotions, slow down and self-reflect on the issue and find something to move you past it. I have had to do this in a few instances, and each time I get better at it and my life gets better for it.

Back in 1999, I merged my company with a larger one. After the merger, I owned 33 percent and my partner owned 67 percent. My partner became a good friend. I looked up to him; I would go so far as to say he became a mentor. We were very different, however, and at the time I was a tad too big for my britches. IA was operational in that I was doing ERP type of work commingled within my responsibilities for our joint company; this work was not in competition but it was in conflict at times, and I was truly wrong for doing both.

After 9/11 we were affected like most other companies. During this time, we decided, because of my recommendation, to invest in another company that was being started by a neighbor. We put a lot of effort into this company too, and it was a big stretch for us. We put our—that is, mostly my partner's—reputation on the line with the bank to make this a go.

Having one partner is tough; two is amazingly difficult. We were growing fast, like seven-figure fast. We did not have the infrastructure needed to maintain the growth, nor did we have experience in such rapid growth. Mistakes mixed with greed and arrogance is never a good combination. Needless to say, the partnership fell apart. The new partner got off without ever having to pay me or my initial partner a dime, something that made me really angry up until 2007. My original partner and I also had a severe falling out. We both ended up financially fine, but not before we both endured tremendous stress and setbacks. The most damaging consequence of all, for me, was the loss of his friendship.

To this day, I miss my original partner. He has become very successful, and I am very happy for him. I split off my original company and today it too realizes amazing success, albeit being run by the people I hired originally as employees, now in full control and ownership. However, despite the money lost—millions—and despite the opportunities lost—millions more—the biggest loss I feel today is the loss of friendship and respect I had for both of the people I started the partnerships with. Money is replaceable; respect can be lost for a lifetime. Protect the respect you earn with all you have, and if you can repair damaged respect by being the bigger person, by all means invest the emotion and time to try.

I have since moved on. Neither of these past partners would extend a hand in greeting today; mine would be left in empty air. I live with a clean conscience knowing that I have paid for my mistakes financially, emotionally, and physically. I also know that when faced with more challenges, I will forever take the high road.

The high road on maintaining respect is my final story. I had partners in my businesses in Oregon. One of them (for the purpose of this story we will call him Partner A) is a wildly successful man who had an original partner (Partner B) in his lifelong business. Partner B also happened to be one of my business partners. I never met Partner B, having only talked to him once on the phone.

Partner B died. His wife was fairly aggressive about wanting to be bought out. During my partnership with Partner A, he taught me about the high road in business. He said, "If you're right, then always follow through regardless of how uncomfortable it is." The best example is how he treated Partner B's wife. They owned property together, and when one of the pieces of jointly owned property was sold, Partner A made sure that the wife of Partner B was paid exactly what was due to her, the moment the property sale closed. Even though there were many unsettled liabilities that far exceeded this amount, he never commingled issues. As he put it, "There is no justification to mixing one piece of business with another; they are not connected except emotionally, and that is not enough to put my reputation at stake."

People so highly respect this man that they will do business with him on a handshake. In a time of litigious behavior and an overabundant demand for contracts to define relationships, he can still be counted on to keep his word. This is the ultimate form of respect that I hope to live by. If I give my word, I strive to keep it. If I don't keep it, I would hope it's because I forgot and not because I consciously decided to not do so. If I ever do make such a mistake, I hope to be held accountable and given the opportunity to make it right.

Situation Awareness

Earning respect from others and holding yourself accountable requires something else that is often difficult to maintain: situation awareness. You can self-reflect and identify those things in your life that challenge and bring you sorrow, grief, and happiness all day, but if you don't have situation awareness about the present, nothing will really change.

Situation awareness is about living in the present and being conscious about what is going on around you. So many of us go through life in that comfortable focus, we miss what is happening around us. Situation awareness is so much more than just knowing what is going on presently. It's about understanding that our behavior and actions, when inconsistent, will breed things in our lives that will give us anxiety.

I delegate to a fault. However, that delegation does not mean I don't pay attention; there is a difference. If you delegate something that you are ultimately in control of, you must find a way to remain aware of that which you delegated. I'm not talking about micromanagement, I'm talking about finding that one thing that will give you enough situation awareness to feel good about being held accountable for that which you have delegated.

The one thing I don't delegate is accountability to our clients. I maintain enough situation awareness to accept that accountability, which at times really sucks. But I never give up more than I can accept responsibility for, and I always try my best to maintain situation awareness to a point where that responsibility never develops into anxiety.

Being aware may mean keeping tabs on project timeliness through dashboards. It may mean having your children check in at certain intervals and meeting their friends. It may be that when you enter into a new place, you take stock of your surroundings and get comfortable enough to focus on why you're there instead of where you are.

Every single time we fly, René pays hyper-attention to the safety briefing; me, not so much. However, in my defense, I fly something like forty to sixty times a year and have for over twenty years, while René flies two or three times a year. Even though René has flown on a Boeing 737 and Airbus 319/320, she still pays attention. Her situation awareness for what to do if there is an inflight emergency is amazing.

However, if you asked René about most of the people around us, she would not be able to tell you much. I am hyper-diligent about those people around me. I want to know who is close to me and what type of people they are. I also consciously tap the seatback of each row between myself and the exit, knowing that should there be an issue I will just have to tap the seatback that number of times to get back to that exit. I use this habit to bolster my innate situation awareness about how to get off the plane without having to listen to the announcement every time I fly.

I have been hyperactive about situation awareness for my entire life. Being situationally aware will also help you to be somewhat intuitive and will help you remain calm during situations that may become stressful.

On the extreme side, there have been a few incidents in my life where situation awareness has helped me stay calm. As you know, in high school I dealt drugs for a number of months to other high school kids. Toward the end of my senior year, when I was doing as many drugs as I was selling, there were a lot of turf battles going on in the drug market. One day I was leaving my friend's apartment, a place where we were known to hang out and party. As I walked from the front door to my car, I noticed a younger person walking toward me, and at the last second as he passed he tried to stick a knife in my chest. My situation awareness allowed me to take the knife in my arm, not my chest, and get out of that situation with only one stab wound.

As an adult, I have been on two airplanes that have had serious issues. The first was in 1996 when an Airbus I was traveling on from Mexico City to Los Angeles decompressed at 36,000 feet. The airplane immediately began a rapid descent, which happened to occur just after some meals had been served; they all hit the roof along with a few people; it was chaos.

The people in my row were calm. The lady next to me grabbed my hand and squeezed; I squeezed back as the airplane did a lazy spiral at a fast rate to a height that would allow us to remove our masks. By the way, the effects of rapid decompression at 36,000 feet feels like someone shoving an icepick between your ears, and you lose the ability to breathe. However, being aware that we were not falling out of the sky and that my seatmates were calm helped me to remain calm and influence the others around me.

This scenario would happen again about three months later on a flight from Denver to Los Angeles; this time, as soon as I could not breathe, I knew what was coming. I used situation awareness once again to remain calm, and once again the influence it had on my seatmates was apparent when compared with the actions of others around us who were quite frankly losing it.

You can apply situation awareness to almost any situation. When I go to my office each day, I try to have situation awareness with regard to my teammates. I look to detect variance in their physical attributes or in their attitudes. Having this awareness of their being helps me to better communicate with them. Using tools to collect data to be situationally aware is also very important.

At IA, we are hired to effect change. We are often tasked with gaining an understanding of the root cause of an issue and then formulating a solution to that issue without upsetting the overall business structure. To accomplish this, we have to be situationally aware of the entire organization. We have developed tools to supply us with situation awareness and help us to be intuitive throughout the process. We call our situation awareness program BizVision. However, the principles we use to collect data are not more complex than just asking a lot of well-designed questions that help us understand that which we are being asked to influence.

If you don't know, ask. If something is not clear, ask for clarification. Situation awareness is about gaining clarity and knowing your surroundings as much as you can. The only way to gain this is to be curious and ask questions.

During your quest for situation awareness, you may become aware of things that are just not quite right. Sometimes it's just perspective, other times it's context. Situation awareness is also knowing if you are being objective or subjective. Just because you like something does not mean it's right. And just because you may be the one in charge does not mean you should use your influence to change things you're subjective about.

Influence

This balance of what we do with our situation awareness leads us to the crux of this book, finding the I in team: Influence.

Influence is the ultimate responsibility we have as humans. What we do with our influence can dramatically alter the outcome of things we may never even know occur. Do you think Abraham Lincoln knew that his influence would lead to the election of an African American president? Do you think those who invented the written word or discovered the principles of mathematics would ever have thought they could influence 7.6 billion humans with a single statement? Or that math would alter the way we look at the world or space?

I could provide examples of good and bad influences and create a separate book. My goal is not to provide comparisons or tell anyone what is right or wrong. My goal is not to give any individual or Individual the tools by which to take advantage in a bad way; we have enough of that going on today. My goal is to make as many people aware that we have an opportunity to influence others, hopefully in a positive way.

If you take the time to slow down your life enough to excel in your chosen fields, I think you will create for yourself the opportunity to be respected and thus have a positive influence on those who meet you. We all have advantages in this life. Those advantages are not the same; they are individual to each of us. Advantages can affect us individually or they can affect us as an Individual group. As I've expressed, Individual Advantages is about each of us individually and each Individual moment, task, or group we live through, accomplish, or work with.

We hear about people individually celebrated; especially in sports. Think about Tom Brady. When you hear about him, you cannot help but be amazed. However, I always wonder, if you put him on the Bears or the Rams instead of the Patriots, would he have the same success? Was his individual advantage that he was part of the Individual team he played with? When you change that team, does the single individual's contribution change? I think it can.

I'm not saying Tom Brady does not deserve credit. He brings to his team an influence that instills in those he plays with the drive to be their very best. The owners of the team continue to surround him with players who complement his advantages, by bringing out the best advantages of his teammates.

At IA, we strive to create organizations in the same context. We help people to understand where they are in the hierarchy; sometimes that is easy, and other times it requires slowing down. In the end, it's all about identifying the influence each person has and how to create the best person to provide the proper influence that will allow the individual to contribute positively.

Influence is that one thing we all have that has the ability to be the most powerful thing we have responsibility for. Influence without accountability can become tyranny. Influence without empathy can become narcissism and totalitarianism. However, influence with empathy and understanding can create a powerful individual who supports the larger Individual that itself has the influence to change lives, directly and indirectly, for a very long time.

As I collect my final thoughts about finding your influence, I am struck by the people who have influenced me. I doubt Jack Danger thought he would ever be influential in the writing of a book like this one. I doubt that my ex-partners would think I would be grateful for the influence they had in my life and will be until my dying breath. I had no idea when I started my company in 1996 that I would have three children and a grand-daughter and would have influenced hundreds of thousands of people around the world with our BizVision process.

When you find yourself struggling with being influenced or influencing others, slow yourself down, be aware of the situation you're in, and try to apply your foundation of self to the problem. Use your influence to gain the best outcome possible to move you forward and add to that which we all seek.

EPILOGUE

Individual Advantages: Be the I in Team (Spring 2019)

The next book will utilize the lessons we have learned here and dive deeper into how you can become the influence you want to be for others. We will, through the same type of lessons (stories), create a path to being influential. Regardless of your goals, we will show you how to apply your new self-understanding to your current situation. We will apply the lessons taught here, and some new ones, to reach new heights.

How did I go from a child with eight homes, to a young man forced to join the Army to get out of going to prison, to leading an organization with influence over hundreds of thousands of people and hundreds of millions of dollars?

What tools do I use, coupled with my self-awareness, to surround myself with individuals who want to follow me on each quest I begin? How do I mentor people to be their very best and keep them focused over a year, two years, or even over twenty years? What allows me to concurrently own and manage, on a daily basis, over forty companies and provide my insight into that ability to hundreds of business owners every year?

To Be the I in Team requires a crystal-clear understanding of who you are on the deepest levels. What you do with that knowledge can be very powerful. *Individual Advantages: Be the I in Team* will lay out the foundation of how you can begin your journey to reaching your goals.

GLOSSARY

advantages: Advantages are the result of who we are; our actions and what we say have influence over everything we interface with.

bandwidth: The capacity of, just about, anything.

comfortable focus: Becoming so accustomed to what we are doing that we no longer think about the act of what we do and just go through the motions. This allows the mind to wander while muscle memory completes tasks.

ERP: Enterprise Resource Planning.

individual: *(characterized by the lowercase i)* A single person, task, or action.

Individual: *(characterized by the capital I)* An entity that is made up of multiple individuals (i.e., families, teams, offices, companies, cities, states, countries, classrooms, groups, etc.).

KPI: Key performance indicators.

opportunity: Advantages that should be "taken advantage of." Opportunities can become advantages.

peanut butter syndrome: When you are so deep in comfortable focus that you do not realize what is right in front of you.

ROI: Return on Investment.

scope creep: Digression from main work objectives.

S.M.A.R.T.: Specific. Measurable. Attainable. Realistic. Timely.

TIADD: Technology Induced Attention Deficit Disorder.

Contact **IA** Business Advisors

For more information about the work Brian and his team provide to clients around the world, visit our website at www.IABusinessAdvisors.com

Visit the book's website: www.FindTheIInTeam.com

Subscribe to our newsletter on our website.

Follow us on social media:

Twitter: IA_Biz_Advisors & IinTeamSeries

Facebook: IA Business Advisors & The I in Team Series

LinkedIn: IA Business Advisors & The I in Team Series

Google+: IA Business Advisors & The I in Team Series

Thank you,
IA Business Advisors